New Zealand's
Native Mammals

New Zealand's
Native Mammals

When and where to see them

CAROLYN KING

A catalogue record for this book is available from the National Library of New Zealand

ISBN 978-1-77694-069-1

A White Cloud Book

Published in 2024 by Upstart Press Ltd.

26 Greenpark Road, Penrose, Auckland 1061

New Zealand

www.upstartpress.co.nz

Text © 2024 Carolyn King

Design and Format © 2024 Upstart Press

The moral rights of the author have been asserted.

Photograph and image copyright © as noted on the Photo Credit Pages

Design and illustration by redinc. Book Design, www.redinc.co.nz

Printed by Everbest, on paper sourced from sustainable forests

Contents

1. Introduction

Most people think of New Zealand as a group of remote South Pacific islands with no native mammals except a few bats. In fact, these islands are only part of a much wider New Zealand Region that includes a large chunk of Antarctica and the Southern Ocean. In that huge area there is, besides the two living resident bat species, a large and vigorous assembly of 57 native marine mammals (3 fur seals, 5 true seals, 1 sea lion and 48 dolphins and whales). This book explains why we have so few land mammals, and, by contrast, celebrates the wonderful diversity of our rich and little-known heritage of native marine mammals.

The unique geography of the New Zealand Region

The modern New Zealand islands comprise the only emergent parts of a large fragment of land and continental shelf known as Zealandia. This land mass began to split off from the rest of the ancient continent of Gondwanaland about 82 million years ago, at a time when Australia and Antarctica were still joined. The areas of Zealandia above sea level were thickly forested and inhabited by representatives of ancient Gondwanaland fauna and flora.

The gap that opened up as Zealandia drifted eastwards, now called the

Map of Zealandia, Earth's submerged 8th continent

Tasman Sea, was more than 1,000 kilometres across by 65 million years ago. Open ocean now stretches much further than that in all directions: 2,388 km north to New Caledonia, 1,500 km west to Australia, 6,252 km south to Antarctica and 9,625 km east to Chile.

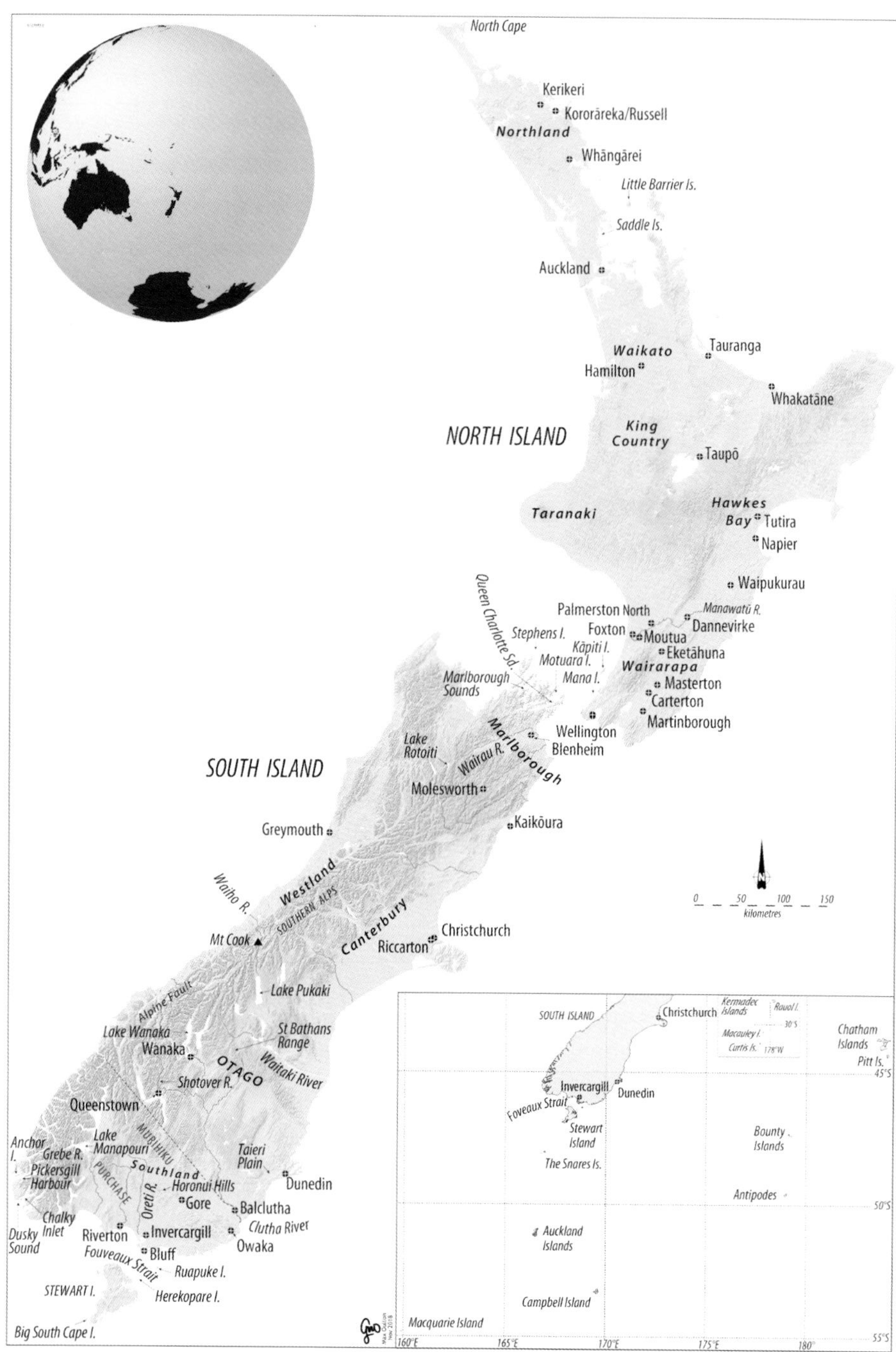
North Cape
Kerikeri
Kororāreka/Russell
Northland
Whāngārei
Little Barrier Is.
Saddle Is.
Auckland
Tauranga
Waikato
Hamilton
Whakatāne
NORTH ISLAND
King Country
Taupō
Hawkes Bay
Taranaki
Tutira
Napier
Waipukurau
Queen Charlotte Sd.
Palmerston North
Manawatū R.
Stephens I.
Foxton
Moutua
Dannevirke
Kāpiti I.
Eketāhuna
Motuara I.
Wairarapa
Mana I.
Marlborough Sounds
Masterton
Carterton
Martinborough
SOUTH ISLAND
Lake Rotoiti
Wellington
Marlborough
Blenheim
Wairau R.
Molesworth
Kaikōura
Greymouth
Westland
Waiho R.
SOUTHERN ALPS
Canterbury
Christchurch
Mt Cook ▲
Riccarton
Alpine Fault
Lake Pukaki
St Bathans Range
Lake Wanaka
Wanaka
OTAGO
Waitaki River
Shotover R.
Queenstown
MURIHIKU
Anchor I.
Grebe R.
Lake Manapouri
Taieri Plain
Pickersgill Harbour
Southland
PURCHASE
Oreti R.
Horonui Hills
Dunedin
Chalky Inlet
Gore
Balclutha
Dusky Sound
Riverton
Invercargill
Clutha River
Owaka
Fouveaux Strait
Bluff
Ruapuke I.
STEWART I.
Herekopare I.
Big South Cape I.
0   50   100   150
kilometres
SOUTH ISLAND
Christchurch
Kermadec Islands
Rauol I.
30°S
Macauley I.
Chatham Islands
Curtis Is.
178°W
Pitt Is.
45°S
Invercargill
Dunedin
Foveaux Strait
Stewart Island
Bounty Islands
The Snares Is.
Antipodes
50°S
Auckland Islands
Campbell Island
Macquarie Island
160°E   165°E   170°E   175°E   180°   55°S

New Zealand's North, South and Stewart Islands (113,729 km², 150,437 km² and 1,748 km² respectively), collectively known as the 'mainland', support a human population of around 5.2 million people across 1,430 km between latitudes 34° and 47° South. The three main islands are only the largest of more than 730 inshore and outlying islands of various sizes larger than 1 hectare. These islands range in size from fragments separated from the mainland coast by narrow channels to scattered larger chunks of land in distant, splendid isolation. Major outlying groups range from the subtropical Kermadec Islands (Raoul and Macauley Islands at 29°S) and the Chatham Islands (800 km east of Christchurch) to the subantarctic groups (Snares, Auckland, Antipodes, Bounty and Campbell Islands, at 52°S). All the islands are fringed by huge expanses of mostly wild coasts, and are surrounded by vast areas of pristine ocean.

Land mammals of New Zealand

The first human voyagers to settle in Zealandia arrived in the late 13th century, and the only living land mammals they found were those whose ancestors had been able to fly from Australia across the Tasman Sea. The early Polynesian colonists found great populations of bats pouring out of caves and tree roosts. At that time, these were the only land mammals living on or visiting the huge forested islands otherwise teeming with birds and reptiles, whose ancestors stretched back to Gondwanan times.

For decades, biogeographers assumed that the reason there are no other living land mammals (or snakes) in New Zealand is that their ancestors all 'missed the boat'. But in fact, the earliest ancestors of all living mammals were already well established in Gondwanaland by 82 million years ago, before Zealandia split away. So the alternative explanation is that there once were pre-modern mammals in New

OPPOSITE: Map showing New Zealand's isolated position in the southwest Pacific Ocean, and the locations of the main and subantarctic islands.

A reconstruction of what the undisturbed forests of Zealandia might have looked like in pre-human times, dominated by birds including two moa; a bat is the only mammal.

Zealand, but they have no living descendants, and we have not yet found any fossils showing that they were ever here.

In 2006, fragments of an until then unknown terrestrial mouse-sized mammal (not an ordinary mouse, nor a marsupial) were found in fossil deposits at St Bathans, in Otago, which were 16–19 million years old. The implication was that tiny land animals belonging to some ancient, mystery species were indeed living on Zealandia at some point after it separated from the rest of the world. But no one has been able firmly to identify them, despite ongoing efforts to find more material. Therefore, there still is not enough evidence to figure out who these enigmatic little creatures might have been or how they fitted into the story of New Zealand's mammal history. The case remains open.

Aside from bats, the forested New Zealand archipelago became, alone among all places on Earth, a land dominated by birds and reptiles. The evolution of terrestrial mammals proceeded in the rest of the world long after all feasible cross-Tasman land connections were lost. All the recognisably modern mammals, round the world and those introduced to New Zealand, are recent by comparison.

Marine mammals of New Zealand

By contrast, the vast majority of mammals native to the New Zealand Region are marine species. The wide, shallow seas of Zealandia's continental shelves have provided rich feeding for a long succession of marine mammals and penguins. The islands' collective coastline of 15,000 km has always been important to land-breeding marine species, hosting seasonal gatherings of breeding fur seals and sea lions, along with thousands of seabirds and penguins, on rocky shores and beaches.

Further out, the rich oceans surrounding the New Zealand islands swarm with marine mammals. Their extreme isolation protected them from human exploitation until James Cook and other early explorers commented on their huge abundance throughout the Southern Ocean and its uninhabited islands. The explorers reported, not only the huge colonies of fur seals and sea lions, but also the extraordinary sight of dolphins and whales romping offshore in their thousands, making them magnets to nineteenth-century sealers and whalers. The survivors of their relentless slaughter are recovering, but are still fewer than they were, and unfamiliar to human observers on shore.

Definitions

Cetaceans — refers to all dolphins and whales generally.
DOC — The New Zealand Department of Conservation, which is

responsible for protecting all native species. DOC's categories of conservation status for native mammal species are shown in Tables 1 and 2.

Clade — a group of organisms comprising all the evolutionary descendants of a common ancestor.

Native — any species whose ancestors evolved in the New Zealand Region or arrived without human help, and which now maintains independent populations in the wild. That means only flying or swimming mammal species that could conquer Zealandia's formidable isolation, i.e., bats, fur seals, sea lions, true seals, dolphins and whales. All are strictly protected.

Endemic — a subdivision of native species that live only in New Zealand or its territorial waters. All species described here are native under the above definition, but only a few are endemic.

New Zealand Region — includes both the island archipelago (total land area of 270,000 km²) and the Ross Dependency (450,000 km²), defined as a sector of Antarctica originating at the South Pole, passing along longitudes 160°E to 150°W, and terminating at latitude 60°S.

Pinnipeds – a collective term for seals and sea lions.

Vagrant — an animal wandering outside its normal geographic distribution.

Why the mammals of New Zealand are unique

The combination of known mammalian species in the New Zealand Region (the 'fauna') is unique in the world. This is the result of New Zealand's peculiar history and geography.

First, the New Zealand Region offers a greater range of habitats and climates than any other biogeographical region in the world. It includes not only a sprawling archipelago of tropical, temperate and subantarctic islands, but also the Ross Ice Shelf and a large section of the Southern Ocean (although Macquarie, Lord Howe and Norfolk Islands are part of the same geographic region defined as part of the Zealandia continent, they are administered by Australia, and are therefore not included among New Zealand's territorial responsibilities).

Second, New Zealand is today the only country in which the non-native terrestrial species are completely dominant (in numbers both of species and of individuals) over the native species. Almost everywhere you travel around New Zealand, the only land mammals you are likely to see will be introduced. This imbalance tends to astound visiting biologists, so one of the purposes of this book is to explain how it came about.

Third, because New Zealand's native species are all by definition good travellers, few are classed as endemic. The longer they have lived isolated from their relatives, the higher up the taxonomic scale their group is placed. Only the longest-resident and most special of all, the short-tailed bats, are endemic at Family level on the taxonomic scale. And only the New Zealand (Hooker's) sea lion is endemic at Genus level, because its isolated main breeding areas lie within New Zealand's section of the subantarctic. The most recently established residents, the New Zealand long-tailed bat, the New Zealand fur seal, and the two separate lineages of the New Zealand (Hector's) dolphin, are endemic at species or subspecies level. No other bats, and few other marine mammals, are confined to the New Zealand region, so the vast majority of marine mammals recognised by the Department of Conservation (DOC) as belonging to the New Zealand fauna are not endemic at any level.

Fourth, New Zealand was the last large land mass to be settled by people. It is the largest by far of the Pacific islands to be colonised by the Polynesians, but also the coldest. Organised settlement by Europeans began a full 50 years after the first convict ships landed their reluctant passengers in Australia. This late start did at least mean that successive New Zealand governments could avoid some of the mistakes made by other colonial powers, including the importation of some of the worst exotic mammalian species that have caused havoc elsewhere. Our acutely vulnerable native bats, lizards and land birds would have been even worse off but for the absence of shrews, field voles, moles, foxes, squirrels and mink. On the other hand, the once enormously abundant marine mammals (especially fur seals and some whales) were once the backbone of early colonial economics, so have suffered decades of ruthless human exploitation.

Innovative technology has been pivotal in the development of current conservation programmes for native mammals. Monitoring programmes and pest management work needs information such as, for example, on how roosting bats can be protected from pests that readily climb trees. Conservation management also needs to address conflicts of interests, such as how to balance the rights of people to go fishing versus the needs of dolphins to be protected from set nets.

How to use this book

This book is intended as a simple guide for anyone interested in discovering the native mammals of New Zealand. Without assuming any prior knowledge, it illustrates and describes the native mammal species that might be seen by New Zealanders and visitors to New Zealand. It includes marine species that might be found cast up on the beaches of the mainland or its offshore and outlying islands, or seen from ships cruising their surrounding seas, or visiting the Ross Dependency in Antarctica.

Species are listed in conventional order, and each group of related species is introduced with a brief list of features they have in common. Each species account includes, where possible, a section headed 'Where to see them', listing the species on open display in the main city museums, and the tourist companies offering mammal watching opportunities. The rich additional information held by local museums is far too extensive to list here, but readers are encouraged to explore them whenever possible.

Measurements are given only broadly, in units appropriate to the size of the animals, and without specifying variation unless there is a large difference between males and females. Similarly, breeding and population data are approximate only. This is sometimes because detailed information does not exist, so what is given may be very rough; more usually, it is because body size, breeding rate and population dynamics of most mammal species are all strongly affected by food supplies, which vary with season, year and social status.

How to view mammals respectfully

New Zealand has a large network of reserves where animals have priority over people. When protected from human interference, animal populations in such places can grow, which makes them magnets for people who want to watch wildlife up close. Be aware that all native wildlife is strictly protected. For terrestrial species, there are provisions for legal consequences of interference under the Wildlife Act 1953. For bats and land-breeding fur seals this includes inadvertent damage such as felling a roost tree or damaging a haul-out site or rookery.

Where to see bats

The forest that once covered 86% of the national land surface has been reduced to 23%. This wholesale forest clearance has had a predictable catastrophic effect on bats, and all other forest-dependent native species.

There are generally no restrictions on viewing living bats in the wild — just so long as people don't disturb them (or fall foul of the Wildlife Act).

Bats can often be seen emerging at sunset from caves near the Mangapohue Natural Bridge on the Ruakuri Track at Waitomo. It's also a good place to bring a handheld bat detector after dark. Grand Canyon Cave near Piopio in the King Country is a good place to view them too —

but it is a nature reserve, so you need to get a permit from DOC to visit.

In the South Island, Talbot Forest (a tiny urban podocarp remnant) in the middle of Geraldine is another good place. The community have been doing predator control there for years, and you can see bats flying on the bush edges at dusk if you are patient. Local experts also take walking tours to see the bats at night at certain times of the year. Timaru District Council are proud of their bats, and have decorated the public toilets in Geraldine accordingly. Try also the lone street light by the Pelorus Bridge, Marlborough, as well as the local camp ground.

Oban, on Rakiura/Stewart Island has three street lights along the waterfront by the school where bats are often seen in summer.

Some wildlife tourist companies offer bat tours, such as Earthlore in the Catlins, but check the internet for the latest information.

For a closer look, all the main museums display mounted specimens representing our two living bat species. The precious fossil remains of extinct species are generally not on display.

Where to see marine mammals

The first six marine sanctuaries specifically devoted to the protection of marine mammals were established between 1993 and 2014. Interest in them has rapidly expanded, so there are now (2024) 44 marine sanctuaries, listed and described on Wikipedia.

In general, the guidelines to watching mammals are simple common sense.

1. Some wild animals become habituated to people, and if usually ignored, they can become tolerant of human activities. Their normal flight reaction is reduced enough to allow humans to approach within sight, at least up to a certain distance. The only wild mammals in New Zealand in this category are fur seals and some dolphins, but even those living

OPPOSITE: Diagram of simple rules for whale watching

Ngā tamariki a Tinirau
Simple rules for interacting with MARINE MAMMALS

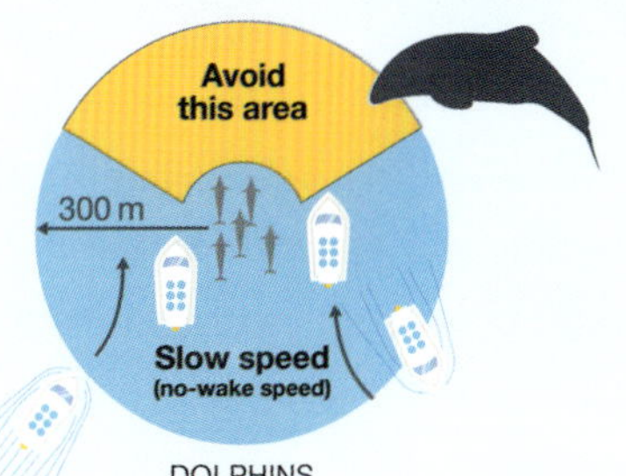

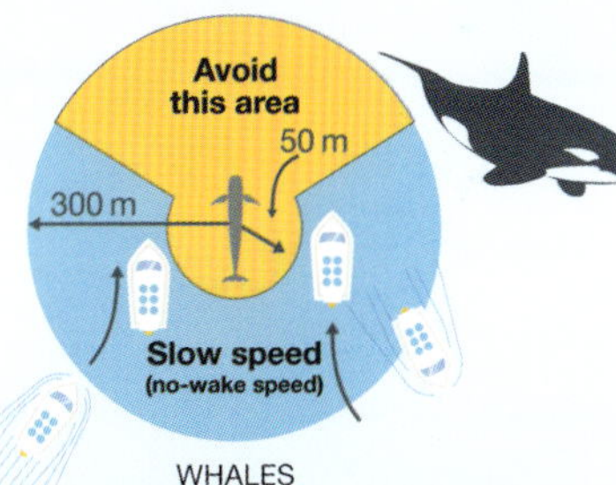

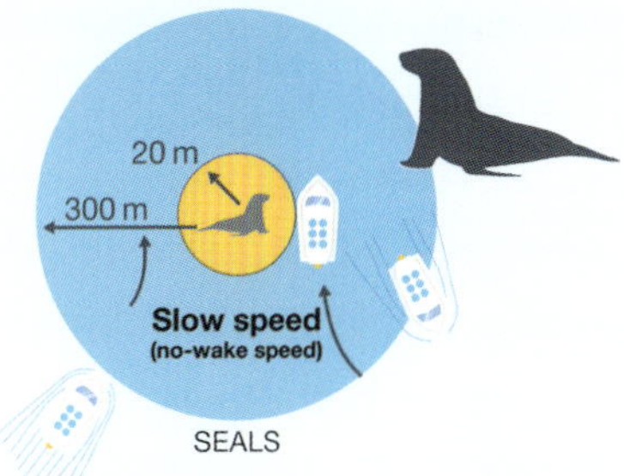

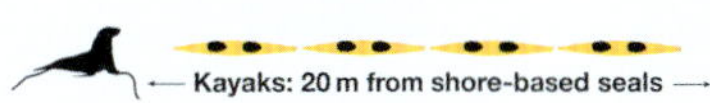

Te whānau puha, ngā aihe me ngā kekeno – e mātaki ai i tai
Whales, dolphins and seals – sea-based viewing

- Ensure you travel no faster than idle or 'no wake' speed within 300 m
- Make sure there are no more than three vessels within 300 m
- Approach from a direction that is parallel and slightly to the rear. Do not circle the marine mammals, obstruct their path or cut through any groups
- Idle slowly away

Ngā aihe
Dolphins

- Gradually increase speed to outdistance dolphins; do not exceed 10 kn until more than 300 m away
- Do not swim with dolphin pods containing juveniles

Te whānau puha
Whales (including orca and pilot whales)

- Stay at least 50 m away from any whale
- Stay at least 200 m away from any baleen or sperm whale mother and calf
- Do not swim with whales

Ngā kekeno
Seals

- Vessels – stay at least 20 m away from the water's edge where seals may be present
- Swimmers – stay at least 5 m away from the water's edge

Ngā kekeno – e mātaki ai i uta
Seals – shore-based viewing

- Stay at least 20 m away
- Do not get between a seal and its escape route to the sea
- Do not handle seals
- Keep dogs away

in the most frequently observed colonies will be disturbed once that invisible threshold is crossed. A very few individuals become positively friendly, like the semi-tame dolphins 'Pelorus Jack' (page 87) and 'Opo' (page 91), or at least more habituated than most, like some elephant seals (page 63). For the rest, the golden rule is to be grateful for their tolerance and keep your distance while watching through binoculars.

2. Most other wild mammals have a fully justified aversion to being approached by people, and flee from them immediately. It's important to avoid frightening them by not invading their personal space, especially in their last refuges of legally protected parks and reserves. If they have pups or mates to guard, or their escape back to sea is blocked, they may become aggressive instead — and an angry seal can run at you faster than you would expect. Any injury you then suffer is your own fault. For responsible whale watching, see page 17.

3. Never offer human food to any wild mammal, because it could change their natural behaviour and would affect their digestion.

4. Wild mammals of any species should never be captured or restrained except by professional wildlife officers, especially not for frivolous purposes such as being included in a selfie photograph. Disentangling cetaceans struggling to free themselves from fishing gear is a dangerous job for specialists. Some seals occasionally haul out on the inhabited mainland (page 50), thereby attracting much local attention, but they should be reported to DOC and thereafter defended from people and dogs, or left alone if possible. For instructions on what to do if you find an entangled or stranded cetacean, see page 19.

Because most of our native mammals are so hard to see in the wild, one excellent way to get a close-up look at them is to visit one or more of our major museums. Those that have displays of named species are listed in this book under each species account. Another way is to join one of the recognised wildlife tourism companies on the internet.

Possible marine mammal watching sites around the New Zealand coast

- Paihia, Northland; Whitianga, Coromandel; Tauranga, Bay of Plenty — Bottlenose and common dolphins.
- Nelson and Picton, Marlborough Sounds — New Zealand and dusky dolphins, orcas and New Zealand fur seals.
- Kaikōura — Sperm whales; New Zealand, dusky and common dolphins; orca, and pilot whales.
- Banks Peninsula Marine Mammal Sanctuary; Greymouth; Te Waewae Bay, South Otago and Curio Bay, Rakiura/Stewart Island — New Zealand dolphins.
- Milford Sound — Bottlenose dolphins, fur seals.

(Note: Local details can change rapidly, so it is important to check online for a current list of certified wildlife tourism and whale watching companies active in New Zealand.)

Strandings

More than 5000 whales and dolphins have stranded on the New Zealand coast since 1840. Baleen whales strand rarely and singly, but toothed whales often and in large groups. DOC responds to an average of 85 stranding incidents a year, usually of single individuals (most often common dolphins, pygmy sperm whales, and beaked whales). Occasional mass strandings involve hundreds, mostly large pods of long-finned pilot whales.

DOC's rescue operations are well organised and often successful, depending on the extent of injuries to the stranded animals. Swift action is vital, so if you find or suspect a stranding, alert the local DOC office immediately, check DOC's website or ring DOC's emergency number 0800 DOC HOT (0800 36 24 68).

A pod of stranded pilot whales on Farewell Spit

Volunteers work to keep stranded pilot whales cool until the tide returns

Whale watching boat

Whale watching

The Marine Mammals Protection Act 1978 and the Marine Mammals Protection Regulations 1992 define how to behave around marine mammals (on land, from the air or at sea), and provide for the complete protection of all marine mammals, whether dead or alive, within New Zealand fisheries waters — that is, within 200 nautical miles (370.4 km) of land. The best opportunities for watching cetaceans are provided by certified tourist companies.

Watching whales from boats or from clifftops has become a major economic benefit of conservation. It is an important part of the tourist industry, growing much faster than tourism in general. Dolphins often ride the bow waves of ships, including the Cook Strait ferries, to the delight of the passengers. Licensed tourist companies offer organised excursions accompanied by knowledgeable guides, focused on the most abundant species that predictably visit their local area. The nine primary locations together attract more than 550,000 visitors a year.

Commercial whale watching began in 1987, and is now the main focus of tourism at Kaikōura. Guides are also able to instruct visitors in the ethics and regulations of whale watching, and discourage human behaviours that disturb the animals. Speeding too close to a whale, or harassing or chasing them, is absolutely forbidden. In New Zealand, no more than three boats may be within 300 m of a whale at any one time, and none closer than 50 m, while swimmers must remain at least 100 m away.

Reporting observations

Mammal watching in New Zealand is not as well supported as bird watching is, which means that almost anything could be worth reporting. Readers of this book are strongly encouraged to contact the Department of Conservation (DOC) to describe whatever they have seen that could be potentially interesting. In particular, any carcass of a native mammal species, any bat roost and, most urgently, any actual or potential strandings of cetaceans, should be reported immediately to the Department of Conservation website at www.doc.govt.nz or call 0800 DOC HOT (0800 362 468).

2. New Zealand's bats

Introduction

The Australian mainland is an island continent with an ancient and diverse fauna, and New Zealand lies downwind of it across the Tasman Sea. The gap between the two land masses began to open in the north around 82 million years ago, and spread southeast-wards to reach over 2,000 km across. The last connection, via the Lord Howe Rise, was cut some 52 million years ago.

Ever since then, the turbulent Southern Ocean has generated many westerly storms that rage around the bottom of the world. They have occasionally caught up helpless birds and bats from Australian airspace and carried them eastwards. A lucky few windblown stragglers found landfall and established new populations.

Of more than 1,400 species of bats in the world, Australia has at least 90. New Zealand has only a handful of living or recently extinct species, all derived from Australian strays. No doubt many others have also been making the trip for tens of millions of years, but we know of only four long-established members of one group (the short-tailed bats, *Mystacina* spp.), and one much more recent and unrelated arrival (the long-tailed bat, *Chalinolobus tuberculatus*).

The only vagrant (or, more likely, a storm-driven waif) we know of that lived long enough to be observed was a small fruit bat, a little red flying fox *Pteropus scapulatus*, which died on landing in about 1926. It was photographed, and its skin nailed up on a barn wall for many years, but the specimen has been lost. It would not have survived for long because New Zealand forests do not supply the foods that fruit bats live on. It is worth mentioning here only because it shows the ongoing potential for windblown bats to cross the Tasman Sea unaided.

Advances in field technology have enabled a huge increase in research on New Zealand bats since the 1990s. Radio transmitters small enough (0.4–0.7 g) to attach to bats that weigh less than 15 g are providing a wealth of information on the natural lives of wild bats for up to a month at a time. Small, handheld, automated heterodyne bat detectors, that record the ultrasonic sounds emitted by bats, have been used throughout the country to study distribution and habitat use. Flying bats can be distinguished with detectors set at approximately 40 kHz for long-tailed bats and 28 kHz for lesser short-tailed bats. There is some overlap between their calls, and the call rate of lesser short-tailed bats is twice as fast as long-tailed bats.

New Zealand's ancient bats

The Mystacinids belong to an ancient family of short-tailed bats originating in Australia at least 40 million years ago. Of the members of the family whose ancestors were windblown across the Tasman Sea by around 35 million years ago, we know of four species. The lesser short-tailed bat is the only one that still survives, with three subspecies. A close relative, the greater short-tailed bat, has declined to probable extinction within living memory, but its loss cannot be proved so it is still classed as Data Deficient. In addition, there are two described and several undescribed extinct species found as fossils.

Evolution in such prolonged isolation has made the New Zealand short-tails different from any other bats in the world. They are therefore all counted as truly endemic species at Family level. They all diverged from their ancestors only in New Zealand, and are found nowhere else. The Australian lineage (known from fossils, the oldest dated to 26 million years ago) is now extinct.

Table 1. Conservation status of New Zealand bats / pekapeka

DOC Category	Common Name	Species
Nationally Critical	Long-tailed bat	*Chalinolobus tuberculatus*
Nationally Vulnerable	Lesser short-tailed bat (northern North Island)	*Mystacina tuberculata aupourica*
At risk — Declining	Lesser short-tailed bat (central North Island)	*M. t. rhyacobia*
At risk — Recovering	Lesser short-tailed bat (South Island)	*M. t. tuberculata*
Vagrant	Little red flying fox	*Pteropus scapulatus*
Data Deficient	Greater short-tailed bat	*Mystacina robusta*

All, except the one vagrant, are endemic to New Zealand.

All Mystacinids are semi-terrestrial. That is, they can be described as 'walking bats'. They save some of the huge energy needed for hunting in flight by spending a lot of time foraging on the ground with their wings tucked into protective pouches. Flying is an expensive way of getting about, so walking was a good hunting strategy in Zealandia's ancient forests. In an environment free from snakes and four-footed mammalian hunters, walking is an option not open to bats native to other countries. The short wingspan and rounded wingtips allow short-tailed bats to take off from the ground, and gives them enough manoeuvrability to navigate between branches through forest interiors, while still capable of fast flight in the open.

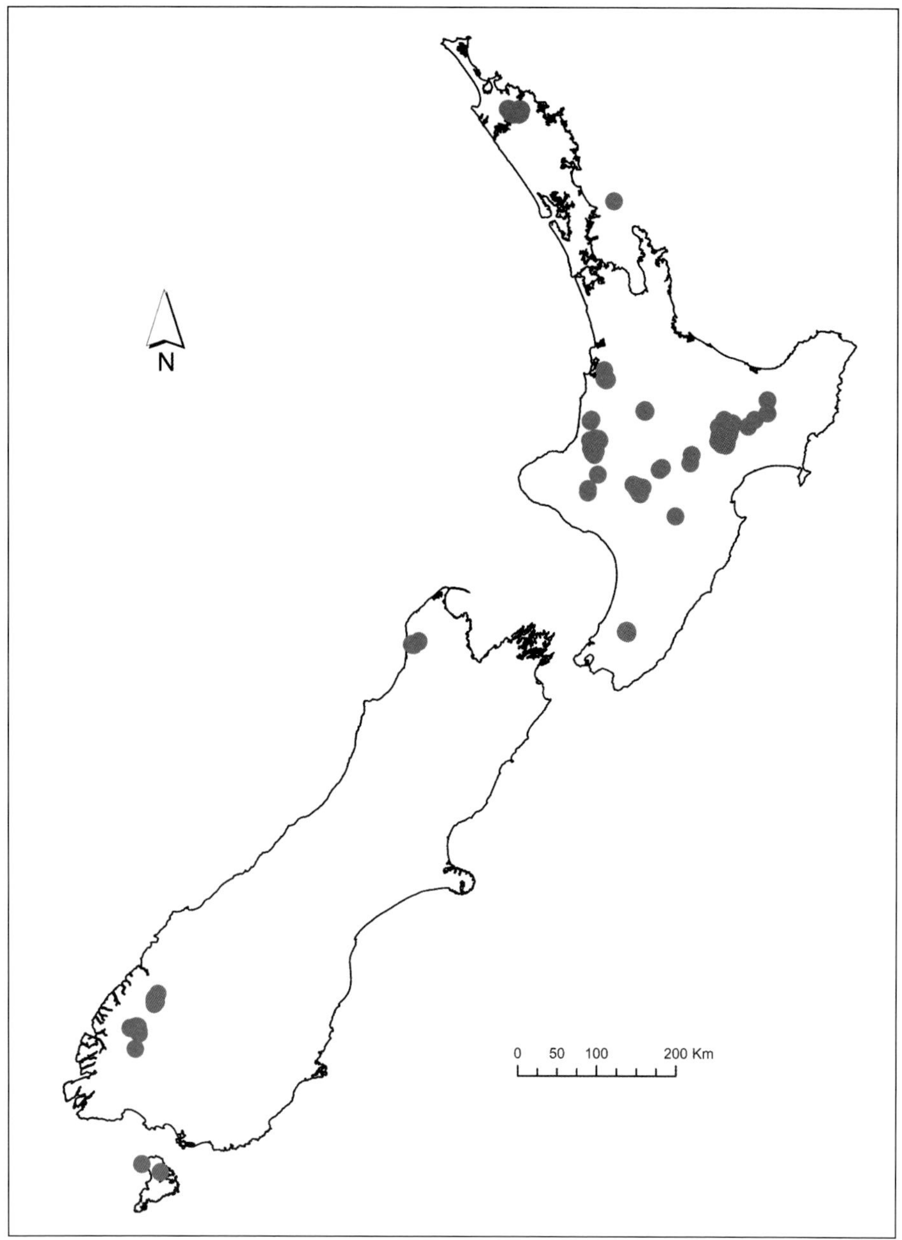

Maps of the present (2000–2018) distributions of New Zealand's living bats. Left, short-tailed bats. Right, long-tailed bats

Lost treasures

We did not know how much more diverse our bat fauna once was until palaeontologists began excavating New Zealand's oldest mammal-bearing sediments in the South Island. Near the village of St Bathans, Otago, is a rich palaeoecological site formed from the ancient bed of Lake Manuherikia, once a vast expanse of fresh water extending across nearly 6,000 km² of the Maniototo Plain of Otago. The sediments have yielded the remains of a huge variety of animals and plants that once lived in and around the lake during the Miocene epoch. The complex community of the time included ancient species such as tuatara, frogs, wrens, kiwi, and early moa. Fossils recovered from that treasure trove have enabled detailed reconstructions of how different life in Zealandia was around 16–19 million years ago. Some of this fossil material will be on display in a special gallery devoted to the St Bathans fossil site in the renovated Canterbury Museum.

Mystacina miocenalis and *Vulcanops jennyworthyae* are large extinct bats, both semi-terrestrial and omnivorous, weighing around 40 g. The structure of their skeletons suggests that they spent much of their foraging time scuttling about on the ground. Their teeth show that both had a broad diet of insects, spiders, wētā, fruit, flowers and nectar. But after the middle Miocene epoch, global temperatures declined from averages up to 12°C warmer than today. The consequent cooling and drying of the atmosphere had drastic effects on the vegetation and environment of all warm-adapted species.

Vulcanops jennyworthyae is different enough from the other Mystacinids to warrant its own Genus. It is the largest member of the four known species of walking bats. Its teeth suggest that it fed on a wide range of food resources, including small vertebrates. It lived on the shores of Lake Manuherikia among a diverse range of other warm-climate Miocene-epoch species, but had disappeared from the fossil record by the end of the Pleistocene epoch.

New Zealand lesser short-tailed bat / pekapeka
Mystacina tuberculata

IDENTIFICATION

The lesser short-tailed bat has short grey-brown velvety fur on the body. The ears, wings, nose, legs, tail are all dark brown and bare. The ears are large (17–19 mm), oval in shape and extend past the nose when held forward. The nostrils are prominent and warty, surrounded by long whiskers, and the eyes are small and dark. In both living and extinct short-tailed bat species, the short tail is partly enclosed within the tail membrane, and partly (7–10 mm) free. The average weight of a lesser short-tailed bat is 12–16 g. The head and body length is 60–70 mm, and the wingspan is 280–300 mm. The only similar species is the New Zealand long-tailed bat,

A mounted specimen of a lesser short-tailed bat in flight, in Te Papa

A lesser short-tailed bat at rest

whose long tail is entirely enclosed in the caudal membrane.

When not in flight, lesser short-tailed bats can fold the wings into a protective pocket under the thicker leading edge, and walk on the wrists and back feet. The forearm, the wrist with a projecting clawed thumb (forming a front 'foot'), the hind legs and the well-clawed hind feet, are all remarkably strong; these bats can scuttle along on all fours almost as rapidly as mice.

The New Zealand lesser short-tailed bat has lived in Aotearoa long enough to have evolved three recognised genetic lineages (Table 1). They differ in geographic distribution, and also slightly in size. The differences between them in appearance do not match their genetic lineages, which muddles the distinction between official subspecies and clades. Nevertheless, these minor differences are important because they reflect

A mounted specimen of a lesser short-tailed bat in walking mode

the long history of short-tailed bats in New Zealand. Their ancestors lived through a very long sequence of drastic landscape changes caused by glaciation and catastrophic volcanic eruptions, inducing a complex series of local extinctions, migrations and recolonisations.

HABITAT

Lesser short-tailed bats need large (over 1,000 ha) blocks of old-growth native forest, including many ancient trees with epiphytes and cavities for colonial roosts. The best roosts are those in internal tree cavities that can maintain a stable, comfortable temperature. Old roosts containing thousands of bats may be located from piles of guano, or the sound of social calls or singing roosts used by courting males. They can tolerate cool weather, so can remain active all year round, but some populations move from high altitude to the lowest available forest in winter. Foraging individuals fly up to 20 km a night, even across open grassland, to reach their favourite foraging grounds.

FOOD

Lesser short-tailed bats have a broad diet, and forage both by echolocation during flight and on the ground by ear and scent. They must eat a third to half of their body weight every night. They have a brushy tongue which can be extended 5 mm beyond the muzzle through a gap between the front teeth. They take insects (beetles, moths, flies, cockroaches and wētā) and nectar, pollen and fruit. They visit large flowers with exposed pollen, and sip accessible nectar from flowers of rātā and pōhutukawa.

The native wood rose (*Dactylanthus taylorii*, an endemic parasitic flowering plant growing on the roots of native trees) produces rich nectar, renewed daily for up to 10 days, and when in flower it provides an important food source for ground-foraging bats. In return, the wood rose depends on bats for pollination. Extinction of one would severely affect the other.

SOCIAL BEHAVIOUR

Lesser short-tailed bats are nocturnal, roosting by day alone or in groups in cavities in old trees or caves. Day roosts are often solitary, but the best colonial roost sites with perceptible thermal advantages are used by large groups. Local populations often have several communal roosts, some occupied for months at a time, others much more briefly. Several large colonies have continued to roost in trees after they have fallen. Their dependence on large communal roost trees makes them especially vulnerable to local catastrophes, as the loss of one such tree hosting 6,000 bats can devastate the local population. Lesser short-tailed bats also pollinate other important forest trees such as pōhutukawa and rātā.

These bats easily slip in and out of short-term (daily) torpor to save energy. In winter they may hibernate for several days at a time, depending on the weather, but less often when huddling in a group.

REPRODUCTION

Lesser short-tailed bats are unusual among bats for using a lek mating system, in which courting males gather to 'sing' near colonial roosts to attract passing females. Males contribute no resources or parental care to their offspring, so all they have to offer is their genetic quality as judged by the females from their singing. Each male's song is different enough that females can distinguish individuals. The mating season is January to May, though most mate in late summer. However, gestation is delayed until spring, October–November, and a single blind, hairless pup is born in December–January, weighing around 5 g.

All pups of a group are gathered in a maternity roost for up to 6 weeks, carried there hanging by their milk teeth from their mother's teat. Pups stay within the maternity roost until they can fly. Mothers roost with them, or at least frequently visit the roost to feed their own pup. Their eyes open and fur grows within about 2 weeks. By 4 weeks old they are fully furred and can fly. By 8 weeks they have grown to full size but are still lighter than adults.

POPULATIONS

The central North Island once supported at least 12.5 million lesser short-tailed bats. Present population estimates range between 30,000 and 50,000 individuals in the largest known groups, scattered over less than 30% of their historical distribution. Total population size estimates (as at 2024) for mature individuals of each subpopulation are:

- Northern lesser short-tailed bat = 1,000–5,000
- Central lesser short-tailed bat = 20,000–100,000
- Southern lesser short-tailed bat = at least 7,000.

The 13 known surviving populations occupy 100–150 km² each, centred on colonial roost trees. The main cause of their decline is deforestation, but introduced predators help to finish off small remnant populations.

Bats were once hunted by the recently extinct whēkau/laughing owl (*Sceloglaux albifacies*), and still are by the living ruru/morepork (*Ninox novaeseelandiae*) and kārearea/falcon (*Falco novaeseelandiae*). For at least the last 120 years, introduced predators have added to the toll, starting with the kiore/Pacific rat (*Rattus exulans*) and domestic or feral cats. After a heavy seedfall in southern beech forests, irruptions of wild house mice increase the number of stoats and rats, usually without distracting their attention from eating native birds and bats. Suppression of these predators in the Eglinton Valley has increased the survivorship of individual bats from 40% to at least 97%. The arrival of ship rats onto Taukihepa / Big South Cape Island in 1963 extinguished lesser short-tailed bats from the island.

The average lifespan and mortality rate of lesser short-tailed bats were long unknown, since armbands used to mark other bats injure the wings of short-tailed bats. But the recent development (since 2006) of passive integrated transponder (PIT tags, also known as microchips) small enough to inject safely under the skin will in due course provide confirmation of other clues that adult lesser short-tailed bats are long-lived.

STATUS

Varies by locality. See Table 1.

WHERE TO SEE THEM

In the field

Lesser short-tailed bats formerly lived throughout all forests of the mainland and Stewart Island, and on most forested inshore islands.

Wholesale deforestation has had a drastic on their populations. Surveys between 1930 and 1960 could still find lesser short-tailed bats on the margins of built-up areas, but since 2005 they have been confined to 13 populations, all in isolated areas of native old-growth forest: one in Northland (Omahuta), one on Hauturu/Little Barrier Island; seven in the central North Island (Urewera, Whirinaki, Pureora, Kaimanawa, Waitaanga, Rangataua and Tahupo); one in the southern North Island (Tararua); and three in the South Island (North-west Nelson, Eglinton Valley, Whenua Hou).

Lesser short-tailed bats fly relatively low and slow, so can be detected moving around a colonial roost with a powerful torch. The high-pitched, rapid chirping songs of lekking males are audible to the human ear from up to 70 metres away.

In museums

Auckland Museum's Origins gallery has a case with two lesser short-tailed bats and one long-tailed bat, taxidermied in flying position. Te Papa's Te Taiao | Nature gallery has a taxidermied lesser short-tailed bat in walking position approaching a wood rose, and a case with bats (unlabelled) taxidermied in flying position. The Canterbury Museum renovation plans to display all New Zealand bats in a special gallery that will reconstruct the prehistory of New Zealand.

New Zealand greater short-tailed bat / pekapeka
Mystacina robusta

IDENTIFICATION

The body of the greater short-tailed bat is similar to that of the lesser short-tailed bat, its smaller relative, but about a third larger and stockier. The average estimated weight of a greater short-tailed bat is about 24 g (none have been weighed, but this is an estimate derived from the normal cubic relationship between length and weight). The head-body length is 70–85 mm, and it has a wingspan of 290–310 mm.

HABITAT

Greater short-tailed bats were once widespread throughout the main islands. The last known population on the Tītī/Muttonbird Islands lived among coastal scrub, in seabird burrows and hollow southern rātā trees, and in sea caves, roosting in sociable colonies. All seabird islands have deep peat forest floors, thick with guano and rich with abundant soil invertebrates. Greater short-tailed bats foraged for insects on the ground, and collected fruits, flowers and the pollen/nectar from rātā. Abundant remains of (presumably roosting) adults and juveniles have also been found on the mainland, especially in Waitomo caves in the Waikato region.

POPULATIONS

The last confirmed specimen was mist-netted on Rerewhakaupoko/ Solomon Island, Southland, in April 1965. The species may be already extinct, but for the moment is still classed as Data Deficient. Searches in 1999 and 2009 were inconclusive.

Subfossil remains in Quaternary period deposits (less than 20,000 years old) on rock ledges, and in swamps sites and limestone caves around Waitomo, Hawke's Bay and Wairarapa in the North Island, and

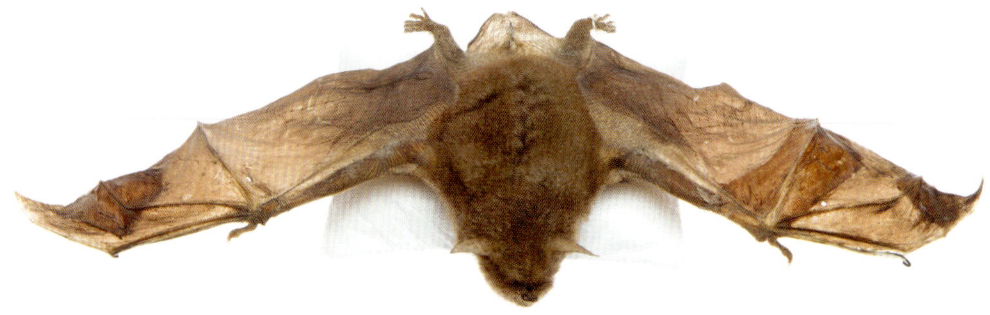

Preserved skin of a greater short-tailed bat

north-west Nelson, Westland, Canterbury and Central Otago in the South Island, have been found co-existing with lesser short-tailed bats.

Laughing owls, morepork and falcons all hunted bats. Both bat species were abundant in the middens of native laughing owls excavated in Nelson and Canterbury, until they were replaced by kiore/Pacific rats (p. 141). The simultaneous exit of greater short-tailed bats from midden records, and the entry of kiore to them, suggests that the kiore was responsible for the loss of these bats from the mainland between 1300 and 1840.

The last remnant population of greater short-tailed bats survived from 1840 until the early 1960s on the Muttonbird Islands. Big South Cape (930 ha), and Solomon Island (32 ha), both lie 2–10 km off the south-west coast of Stewart Island (adjacent to the rat-free islands off the west coast of Stewart Island). Ship rats arrived in the early 1960s and reached plague numbers by 1964–67. Reports of bats seen around their roosting cave fell rapidly, from hundreds in the Puai Cave on Big South Cape in 1961 to few in 1965 to none in 1966.

STATUS

Their Data Deficient rating means that DOC is not prepared to rule out the chances that some unknown relict population might yet be found. See Table 1.

WHERE TO SEE THEM

Greater short-tailed bats are extinct on the mainland, and probably on offshore islands too, but searches continue. Auckland Museum and Canterbury Museum both have skins collected from one of the last known colonies on Solomon Island, both shown with wings spread. Te Papa has a specimen preserved in spirits. None of these precious specimens are on open display.

New Zealand long-tailed bat / pekapeka
Chalinolobus tuberculatus

The long-tailed bat is the only other species of living bat in New Zealand. Its ancestors arrived much more recently than those of the Mystacinids, and it represents an entirely different bat Family. It evolved in New Zealand from an Australian species of *Chalinolobus* that arrived unaided sometime during the early Pleistocene epoch, within the last million years. It is distinct from its Australian relatives, so is endemic to New Zealand, but only at the species level. It is classed as Nationally Critical.

IDENTIFICATION

The fine, soft fur of females is a rich chestnut colour, whereas males are darker, with pale underparts in both. The limbs, wings and tail membrane are all naked and black. The long tail is entirely enclosed in the tail membrane. The head has a high forehead, small eyes, and short, broad ears with a fleshy lobe on the lower ear margin and at the corner of the mouth. A

A long-tailed bat showing the position of its identification tag

small thumb with a long, curved claw projects from the wrist, half way along the wing. The wing is strong enough to support a tiny metal identification tag. The only similar species is the lesser short-tailed bat, which has the last 7 mm of the tail free of the caudal membrane. In flight the two can be distinguished by their different echolocation calls recorded by bat detectors.

Long-tailed bats are small and delicate, weighing 7–12 g, with a head-body length of 42–63 mm and a wingspan of 240–300 mm. Breeding females are larger than males.

HABITAT

Long-tailed bats can live in all types of native forest, from sea level to tree line, and on the less-developed urban fringes of some cities, notably Hamilton and Auckland. They can also be found in some exotic forests, where they forage along the straight-line canopy breaks cut by roads. In native forests they feed close to patch edges and above the canopy rather than in the cluttered interior. Along the habitat edges provided by roads, activity of long-tailed bats declines as overnight traffic rates increase, but not along edges 200 metres or more distant from the roads. The activity rates of long-tailed bats in and around Hamilton city are highest in areas with low densities of streetlights, housing and roads.

They prefer to roost in small, dry, well-insulated cavities well above ground level, such as knotholes or rock crevices in cliff faces. They avoid most large, chilly caves, even where caves are common.

FOOD

Long-tailed bats fly fast, and deftly catch insects on the wing by echolocation. They prefer craneflies, moths and beetles. Temperature, wind strength, cloud cover, moonlight and the activity of invertebrates influence when and for how long long-tailed bats fly each night. Radio-tagged long-tailed bats in the Eglinton Valley make on average four foraging flights, interspersed with three roosting periods, per night.

The wing of a long-tailed bat

Temperature and humidity during the first four hours after sunset help to predict the likely amount of activity through the night. In cold weather they save energy by slipping into torpor during the day, when their body temperature can fall to within a few degrees of external ambient, and energy expenditure can be reduced to about 2% of normal. Survival is highest in the best habitats, which provide the safest, warmest roost sites, and where individuals can reach the best condition.

SOCIAL BEHAVIOUR

Long-tailed bats are nocturnal and sociable, living in complex and variable groups of all ages that can number in the hundreds. Individuals of both sexes switch frequently between solitary and colonial roosts. The foraging ranges of neighbouring social groups overlap. Members of smaller subgroups roost together or alone, often changing group composition and moving almost daily between roosting sites. Home ranges are measured in hundreds of hectares.

REPRODUCTION

Females over 2–3 years old produce a single pup in November–December. The female can carry her non-flying young until they exceed 80% of her body weight. The young bats can fly by about 5–6 weeks old.

POPULATIONS

Morepork/ruru owls and the extinct laughing owl/whēkau are, or were, the natural predators of long-tailed bats, but had no effect on bat numbers throughout New Zealand in the 1800s. Fortunately, these bats are surprisingly long-lived for such small animals. In the Eglinton Valley, the oldest known wild female was >26 years old in 2024, and the oldest male 22 years old. Three colonies in the valley averaged 303 banded individuals in total, plus there were another five colonies in the valley, implying that the local population was more than 800 individuals. Before any invasive predators arrived, population sizes would have been significantly greater. Now, survival is lowest during post-seedfall rodent irruption years when stoats and ship rats are abundant.

Possums and rats in forests, and pigeons, sparrows and wasps on cliff faces, exclude bats from otherwise suitable roost sites. Domestic cats have been known to bring home freshly-dead remains of bats in Cambridge and Hamilton. One particular domestic cat near Geraldine killed three long-tailed bats under an outside house light, where the bats were apparently feeding on moths attracted to the light. Several roost trees, reported to contain 'hundreds' or 'thousands' of bats, were cut down in the nineteenth century, and more are still being reported.

STATUS

See Table 1.

WHERE TO SEE THEM

In the field

Long-tailed bats are still widely distributed on the mainland and on Stewart, Great Barrier, Little Barrier and Kapiti Island forests, but are now rare or absent at many sites where, even as late as the mid-1980s, they were still common, especially on the eastern South Island around Geraldine. In Grand Canyon Cave, an unusual cave-based night roost, up to around 360 bats may enter the cave on one night.

In museums

There are five taxidermied skins of bats in flight mode on display in Te Papa's Te Taiao | Nature gallery, and one in Auckland Museum's Origins gallery.

3. New Zealand's marine mammals

The New Zealand archipelago is an array of isolated chunks of land surrounded by shallow seas that cover the broad continental shelf of Zealandia. The emergent parts of Zealandia still amount to only about 6% of the total 49 million km² continental shelf, but its peculiar geography has made it one of the best places in the world to study the diversity and evolutionary history of marine mammals.

The living taxa of New Zealand marine mammals are listed in the following table by their conservation status, as determined by DOC in 2019. Not all species listed by DOC are discussed in this book.

Table 2. Conservation status of New Zealand's marine mammals.

DOC category	Common name	Species
Otariids / Eared seals (4)		
NR Vagrant	Antarctic fur seal	*Arctocephalus gazella*
Not threatened	New Zealand fur seal*	*Arctocephalus forsteri*
NR Vagrant	Subantarctic fur seal	*Arctocephalus tropicalis*
Nationally Vulnerable	New Zealand sea lion*	*Phocarctos hookeri*

* = Endemic
NR = Non Resident

Table 2. Cont.

DOC category	Common name	Species
Phocids / Earless seals (5)		
Nationally Critical	Southern elephant seal	*Mirounga leonina*
Naturally uncommon	Leopard seal	*Hydrurga leptonyx*
NR Vagrant	Weddell seal	*Leptonychotes weddellii*
NR Vagrant	Crabeater seal	*Lobodon carcinophagus*
NR Vagrant	Ross seal	*Ommatophoca rossi*
Cetaceans / whales, dolphins, porpoises (48)		
Threatened (5)		
Nationally Critical	Bryde's whale	*Balaenoptera brydei*
Nationally vulnerable	South Island New Zealand dolphin / Hector's dolphin*	*Cephalorhynchus hectori hectori*
Nationally Critical	Māui's dolphin*	*Cephalorhynchus hectori maui*
Nationally Critical	Orca	*Orcinus orca*
Nationally Endangered	Bottlenose dolphin	*Tursiops truncatus*
At Risk — Recovering (1)		
	Southern right whale	*Eubalaena australis*
At risk — Naturally uncommon (1)		
	False killer whale	*Pseudorca crassidens*

Table 2. Cont.

DOC category	Common name	Species
NR Migrant (1)	Humpback whale	*Megaptera novaeangliae*
NR Vagrant (6)		
	Pygmy killer whale	*Feresa attenuata*
	Killer whale	*Orcinus sp. Type B*
	Killer whale	*Orcinus sp. Type C*
	Killer whale	*Orcinus sp. Type D*
	Melon-headed whale	*Peponocephala electra*
	Offshore pantropical spotted dolphin	*Stenella attenuata attenuata*
Not threatened (4)		
	Common dolphin	*Delphinus delphis*
	Long-finned pilot whale	*Globicephala melas*
	Dusky dolphin	*Lagenorhynchus obscurus (unnamed subsp.)*
	Gray's beaked whale	*Mesoplodon grayi*
Data deficient (30)		
	Antarctic minke whale	*Balaenoptera bonaerensis*
	Sei whale	*Balaenoptera borealis*
	Pygmy blue whale	*Balaenoptera musculus brevicauda*
	Southern/Antarctic blue whale	*Balaenoptera musculus intermedia*
	Fin whale	*Balaenoptera physalus*
	Arnoux's beaked whale	*Berardius arnuxii*
	Pygmy right whale	*Caperea marginata*

Table 2. Cont.

DOC category	Common name	Species
	Short-finned pilot whale	*Globicephala macrorhynchus*
	Risso's dolphin	*Grampus griseus*
	Southern bottlenose whale	*Hyperoodon planifrons*
	Pygmy sperm whale	*Kogia breviceps*
	Dwarf sperm whale	*Kogia sima*
	Fraser's dolphin	*Lagenodelphis hosei*
	Hourglass dolphin	*Lagenorhynchus cruciger*
	Southern right whale dolphin	*Lissodelphis peronii*
	Andrews' beaked whale	*Mesoplodon bowdoini*
	Dense-beaked whale	*Mesoplodon densirostris*
	Ginkgo-toothed beaked whale	*Mesoplodon ginkgodens*
	Hector's beaked whale	*Mesoplodon hectori*
	Strap-toothed whale	*Mesoplodon layardii*
	True's beaked whale	*Mesoplodon mirus*
	Lesser/pygmy beaked whale	*Mesoplodon peruvianus*
	Spade-toothed whale	*Mesoplodon traversii*
	Spectacled porpoise	*Phocoena dioptrica*
	Sperm whale	*Physeter macrocephalus*
	Striped dolphin	*Stenella coeruleoalba*
	Rough-toothed dolphin	*Steno bredanensis*
	Shepherd's beaked whale	*Tasmacetus shepherdi*

Table 2. Cont.

DOC category	Common name	Species
	Goose-beaked whale	*Ziphius cavirostris*
	Dwarf minke whale	*Balaenoptera acutorostrata 'dwarf''*

The large DOC category 'Data Deficient' includes species that are definitely present at least intermittently, but for which key life history data are unknown.

One further species not listed in this table is Ramari's Beaked Whale (*Mesoplodon eueu*) named after Ramari Stewart.

PINNIPEDS

Introduction

The Otariidae (fur seals and sea lions) and the Phocidae (true seals) are both derived from a common ancestor that lived in the early Miocene epoch, 20–28 million years ago. They have many features in common, so are collectively known as the pinnipeds ('fin-foots').

The earliest ancestors of the modern pinnipeds appeared in the Southern Ocean much later than the cetaceans (dolphins and whales), and their fossils are rare. The lack of older fossils was once thought to mean that seals and sea lions evolved in the northern hemisphere and were slow to migrate southwards. But several important fossils found only recently have changed our understanding of the origins of the pinnipeds.

The earliest New Zealand fossil of a true seal was excavated from a rich deposit of marine fossils of Pliocene age dated to 3–3.4 million years ago, found on the coast of Taranaki. It lived in southern waters about 3 million years ago and later crossed the equator northwards. It was named

Eomonachus belegaerensis — the 'dawn monk seal from Belegaer' (the western 'Great Sea' from Tolkien's Middle Earth, whose unofficial home is also in New Zealand). This fossil suggests that the ancestors of the northern hemisphere monk seals evolved in the southern hemisphere.

The earliest New Zealand fossil sea lion known so far is *Neophoca palatina*, found as a nearly complete adult male skull on Ōhope Beach on the North Island in 1937. It is similar to, but distinguishable from, the Australian seal lion *N. cinerea*, and is of Pleistocene age.

Otariidae / eared seals

Fur seals and sea lions have sleek, streamlined bodies, small ears and long whiskers. They are beautifully agile in water, but they can also move fast on land. They support their weight mainly on their large fore-flippers, and climb remarkably well across rocks, using their hind flippers turned forward like back feet. Males compete fiercely for breeding rights, so are always much larger than females. Haul-out (resting) sites on land are used most often in winter and spring, and rookeries (breeding sites) are used in summer (November to January).

Males and females aggregate only once a year, so females must mate again immediately after giving birth. The gestation period is much shorter than a year, so the embryo goes into diapause for several months, reawakening to continue active gestation in time to reach full term by next pupping season.

New Zealand has two resident species of eared seals, the Southern fur seal (*Arctocephalus forsteri*) and the New Zealand/Hooker's sea lion (*Phocarctos hookeri*).

New Zealand fur seal / kekeno
Arctocephalus forsteri

IDENTIFICATION

The pelt is dark grey-brown, with a silvery sheen over dense underfur when dry. Males have massive thick necks and a heavy mane. The pointed snout is equipped with long, luxuriant whiskers. The eyes are large and brown with no tear duct, so the fur below the eye is constantly wet. Hearing and sense of smell are more acute than sight, especially for females to identify their own pups.

SIZE

Adult males average 125–150 kg, and females are 40–50 kg. Pups are 3–4 kg at birth.

NEW ZEALAND DISTRIBUTION

This is the only one of eight species of southern fur seals classed as permanently resident in the New Zealand Region. Genetic analyses suggest that there are three non-exclusive breeding groups, based around the coasts of New Zealand, Australia and the subantarctic islands. Since the end of commercial sealing, recolonisation of the depleted New Zealand populations has come mainly from remote western colonies.

Virtually all subantarctic islands have breeding colonies that have been used by generations of seals. In addition, many new haul-out sites and rookeries have appeared around mainland coasts in the last 40 years, mostly on the South Island, but now also (after a long absence) on the southern North Island. Their thick fur insulates them equally well either when swimming in cold water, or hauled out in raw, chilly climates.

HABITAT

Their preferred habitat is coastal, plus a limited range out to sea. They favour exposed rocky coasts less favoured by sea lions, with shallow pools for adults to cool off and for pups learning to swim. Non-breeding fur seals have few requirements other than easy access to haul-outs, particularly where they have habituated to people, for example on Muaupoko/Otago Peninsula. Typical foraging dives range from 40 to 200 metres, of 3–15 minutes duration.

FOOD
Squid, octopus, fish, penguins.

SOCIAL BEHAVIOUR
Males come ashore first, establish territories in October–November, and defend them against rival males by vigorous chest-pushing or face-slashing contests. This may go on, if necessary, for weeks at a time without eating. Defeated males break off encounters by ceasing

Head of a fur seal, showing its long whiskers

A group of fur seals resting on the water

aggressive behaviour, emitting submissive screeches and backing away. They are then often forced to leave the colony through a barrage of bites from neighbouring territorial males. Females choose the best territories to produce their pups, and afterwards mate with the territory owner. Some males collect several females, others none. Challenges to the haves by the have-nots continue all season, until the end of the birthing/mating season in January, when the exhausted males return to sea.

REPRODUCTION

Females mature at 4–6 years. They are sexually receptive for only about 24 hours in December–January. After fertilisation, at approximately 8 days postpartum, embryos develop to the blastocyst stage, and then go into diapause until implantation in April or May. Active gestation is only 7 months.

A fur seal resting on a rocky beach

The pups are born in December at 3–5 kg, fully furred and with their eyes open. Mothers and pups learn each other's scent and calls immediately, and thereafter reject contact with all others. Mothers suckle their pups for approximately 12 days, then intermittently between gradually lengthening foraging trips. By June, when the pups have been unable to suckle for many days at a time, they may spend a third of their time suckling on their mother's first day back from a foraging trip. Most pups are weaned in September, some later.

The maximum known age for males, estimated from counts of the annual growth layers in the roots of their teeth, is 15 years, and 22 years for females.

COMMERCIAL SEALING

During the peak of industrial sealing (1810–1830), fur seals were devastated by European and American sealers because of the great value of their fine, dense underfur. All accessible populations were practically exterminated by ruthless, uncontrolled, indiscriminate slaughter from ships capable of reaching all known mainland and subantarctic populations. At least 7 million seals were killed by 1833, but commercial competition ensured that many sealing locations were kept secret and/or their records falsified. Closed seasons were imposed 1875. In 1916, fur seals were protected and all sealing was stopped.

The New Zealand Marine Mammals Protection Act 1978 now prohibits killing fur seals directly, but cannot prevent them from being incidentally captured in trawl nets.

PRESENT POPULATIONS

Mainland breeding groups were formerly hunted by sea lions, and also for meat by Māori, to local but not total extinction. Now they are recolonising many of their former mainland and island strongholds, steadily recovering and reclaiming much of their former distribution. The present estimate suggests at least 75,000 in New Zealand, plus thousands more resident in Australia.

Over the 10-year period from 2002–03 to 2011–12, 1,008 fur seals were observed to be caught in trawl fisheries in New Zealand waters, including 82 in the 2011–12 fishing year alone. At sea they are vulnerable to sharks and leopard seals.

STATUS

DOC Resident Native, Not threatened. IUCN Least Concern. Listed under Appendix 11 of the Convention on International Trade in Endangered Species of Wild Fauna and Flora (CITES).

A 19th century sealing gang in action

WHERE TO SEE THEM

In the field

Fur seals are increasingly valuable to tourism, and kayak-based and swim-with-seals programmes are popular, especially in Abel Tasman National Park and at Kaikōura. All tourist operations deliberately approaching seals are required to hold a Department of Conservation (DOC) Marine Mammal Permit.

There are large rookeries on Cape Saunders, Cape Foulwind and Banks Peninsula. Groups of pups can sometimes be seen practising their swimming in the pool below the waterfall at Ōhau Point. The best time to see them is October–March when the bull seals return to mate and the pups are at their most playful. Auckland Zoo has some rescued fur seals.

In museums

Tūhara Otago Museum's Nature gallery has a large adult fur seal mount standing in an upright position, and a juvenile mounted in a swimming position, accompanied by a skeleton in the same pose. There is also a mount of a pup in Tūhara Otago Museum's Animal Attic.

New Zealand sea lion / Hooker's sea lion / pakake / whakahao
Phocarctos hookeri

IDENTIFICATION

Males are dark brown, and females creamy-grey to white. Pups are born dark brown, but moult to silver-grey. Older males become progressively darker, while females remain pale. Adult males have a thick, coarse mane. Otherwise the coat of both sexes is sparse with no underfur. The blunt snout has long whiskers.

SIZE

The New Zealand sea lion is much larger than the fur seal. Adult males average 320–450 kg and females 85–160 kg. Pups are 7–8 kg at birth.

NEW ZEALAND DISTRIBUTION

This species is found only in New Zealand waters — not (unlike the fur seal) in Australia, where it is replaced by another sea lion, *Neophoca cinerea*.

Sea lions once ranged around all mainland coasts right up to the northern North Island and to the Chatham Islands. Prehistoric remains up to 10,000 years old have been reported from at least 47 sites from North Cape to Stewart Island, and as far east as the Chatham Islands. Intense harvesting has limited their distributions further and further southwards over time. Now the main breeding sites are on sandy beaches in the Auckland Islands group (Enderby Island, Dundas Island, and Figure of Eight Island in Carnley Harbour), plus Campbell Island. Wandering males often visit the southern coasts of Otago and Stewart Island, and a thriving new breeding colony is developing around Dunedin.

HABITAT

Flat sandy beaches, coastal dunes and forest up to 1 km from shore. Sea lions forage in shallow water over the continental shelf. Average dives last 3–4 minutes, to around 120 metres, up to maximum dives of 11 minutes and 500 metres.

FOOD

Octopus, fish, occasional seabirds, penguins and fur seal pups.

SOCIAL BEHAVIOUR

Adult males haul out in October–November and establish territories of around 5 metres diameter. They defend their territories by ritual posturing, charging, and fierce fighting. Only the largest few (about 20%) of territorial males get to breed.

Females arrive in December, about two days before giving birth. They congregate in companionable groups on the beach until near parturition, then isolate themselves for birth.

REPRODUCTION

Females produce their first pup at 4 years old, then average two pups every three years. Males mature at 5, but seldom breed until 8–10 years

Male and female sea lions

old. Females produce pups alone, most over a short two-week period between mid-December and mid-January. They establish an immediate bond with their pup by smell and voice. They suckle it for around 10 days, mate again with the nearest territorial male, then return to sea for a first short foraging trip.

Pups over 10 days old gather in groups on the beach while their mothers are away. Mothers return frequently to suckle, mainly, but not only, their own pup. At 4–6 weeks, mothers move their pups to shelter inland, returning to suckle them at gradually lengthening intervals. Pups learn to swim in inland streams or tidal rock pools, then are led to sea by their mothers in February. Lactation continues until the pups are about 10 months. Adults can live to 28 years old.

POPULATIONS

Māori hunting eradicated all historic mainland populations by AD 1450, but their absence permitted the northward expansion of a related but distinct lineage of sea lions that had previously been confined to subantarctic islands. The lack of dense underfur made sea lion pelts less attractive to European sealers, but after about 1815 they were accepted as substitutes for the rapidly disappearing fur seals. All populations of both were reduced to remnants by the mid-1830s.

Sea lion numbers slowly increased after all sealing ended in 1916, but since the late 1990s their numbers have been significantly declining. Only 2,316 pups were born in 2015, a decrease of 13% since 1995 and a 27% decline since the highest pup production estimate in 1998. The losses have been driven by a 48% decline in productivity at the Auckland Island main breeding area since 1998. By contrast, there has been a slow but gradual increase in pup numbers born on the Otago Peninsula / Catlins area since 1992. The New Zealand Sea Lion Trust records the arrival on the mainland of the first female, born on the Auckland Islands in the late 1980s. She produced 11 pups before disappearing in 2010. Pup numbers born on the mainland have increased as her descendants have reached maturity and begun breeding.

Ongoing high mortality is attributed to epidemic disease (53% of pups on Auckland Island died in January 1998) and to trawling by-catch (1,322 sea lions were killed in the Auckland Islands squid fishery 1992–2009). An adaptive rule defines a maximum allowable by-catch which, when exceeded, can require the squid fishery to be closed early. However, even with these measures, the sea lion population has continued to decline, and fishery-related mortality is still considered the most significant negative impact on the species. The total surviving population is estimated at about 12,000.

STATUS

DOC Endemic, Nationally Vulnerable. IUCN Vulnerable.

WHERE TO SEE THEM

In the field

Haul-outs used mainly by males, especially in winter, are found on the coasts and offshore islets of Stewart Island and the South Island. Pups can be seen at regular rookery sites on Otago Peninsula, Waipapa Point, Surat Beach, Cannibal Bay, Port Pegasus and Stewart Island.

The same restrictions on tourist activities on the mainland apply as for fur seals, but sea lions are much less commonly seen. The main subantarctic rookeries can be observed only from boats operated by specialised tourist companies.

In museums

Tūhara Otago Museum's Animal Attic has a full mount of a sea lion standing with its body raised up on its flippers, and a skull with mandible.

Phocidae / true seals

True seals have no external ears, and cannot turn their hind flippers forward, so they can move on land only by a series of inelegant humping motions like a caterpillar. New Zealand has five species of true seals. Of these, elephant seals and leopard seals are the most likely to visit the New Zealand mainland; the other three are usually confined to the Antarctic, but are rarely recorded as vagrants in New Zealand waters. Males are much larger than females only in species that have stable breeding colonies and vigorous competition between males for mating rights. All use delayed implantation to synchronise parturition among females.

Southern elephant seal / ihu koropuku
Mirounga leonina

IDENTIFICATION

Pups are born with black fur, turning silvery-grey by three weeks. The adult hide is dark grey with short, stiff hair and no underfur overlying a massive layer of blubber. Males have large canines and a huge inflatable proboscis on the nose. Both sexes suffer 4–6 weeks of catastrophic full moult (females and juveniles November–January, and males January–March), when they lie in muddy wallows sloughing off hair and skin in large patches, at huge energy cost in enforced fasting and skin regrowth. When at sea, they dive for 20 minutes on average, to a maximum of 2 hours. Dives are usually down to 400 metres, but often to 1,000 metres.

SIZE

Male southern elephant seals are the largest seals in the world, averaging 3,500 kg, and females average 500 kg. Pups weigh about 40 kg at birth.

NEW ZEALAND DISTRIBUTION

Of the four main genetically independent breeding stocks spread around

Mating elephant seals

the Antarctic, one has rookeries on Campbell and Antipodes Islands. Individuals visit Auckland, Snares, Stewart, Chatham and eastern South Island (Nugget Point), and occasionally produce pups there.

HABITAT

Beaches, dunes and easily accessible flat coastal areas.

FOOD

Squid, octopus, and fish, including deep-water species.

SOCIAL BEHAVIOUR

Males haul out in late August, but do not hold territories. They compete fiercely, mostly by posturing and roaring, or (rarely) in fights where they inflict gruesome injuries on each other until a dominance hierarchy is established. Dominant males, which are up to 10 times the weight of females, herd females into harems and achieve most matings. However, females will also mate with other males, so many pups are not sired by the dominant male of the local group.

REPRODUCTION

Females haul out just before parturition in September. They suckle their pup on very rich milk for about 3 weeks, mate again in early November, then return to sea after a total of 4 weeks' fasting ashore. Implantation of the blastocyst is delayed for 5 months. Pups can triple their birth weight before their mother leaves, then live for 5–6 weeks on stored fat while learning to swim, and leave for sea in December. Females mature at 4–7 years, then breed annually to 12–15 years old, some to age 20. Males mature at 5 years, but few young males under 12 years old can hold a harem, and most do not survive that long.

POPULATIONS

Intensive harvesting for blubber oil ended in the New Zealand Region in 1830. The surviving New Zealand breeding population on Campbell Island was numbered at 417 in 1947, but has since been reduced by 97%. Pup production there has declined from 191 in 1947 to 5 in 1986. By contrast, the South Atlantic population is large (over 460,000) and growing.

STATUS

DOC Nationally Critical. IUCN Least Concern.

WHERE TO SEE THEM

In the field

Some known individuals become regular visitors on the mainland. 'Humphrey' hauled out on Coromandel/Bay of Plenty every summer for 5 years to 1989–90, visiting a dairy farm and a caravan park, causing consternation (and some danger) to cows and campers. Likewise, 'Homer' was seen over several years to 2000 at Christchurch, then Gisborne. Visits by tour ships to Antarctic rookeries are strictly controlled under the Antarctic Treaty.

In museums

Tūhara Otago Museum's Animal Attic has a sagittal section of a skull in a wall case.

Weddell seal
Leptonychotes weddellii

IDENTIFICATION

The body and most parts of the flippers are thickly furred, blue-black above and spotted with white on the belly. The head is small in proportion to the large body, with a short muzzle and whiskers, and large deep-brown eyes. The incisors and canines are strong and project forward into an efficient ice reamer used for keeping breathing holes open throughout winter.

SIZE

Both sexes vary between years, usually 350–500 kg. Pups average 24 kg at birth.

NEW ZEALAND DISTRIBUTION

Ross Ice Shelf, McMurdo Sound, Ross and White Islands, and throughout the Ross Sea. Recorded as vagrants in New Zealand waters five times between 1926 and 2007.

HABITAT

Most live on the fast ice (up to 3 metres thick, extending 400 km from the coast in winter), also ranging to the edge of the pack ice. They haul out on the ice surface alongside the spaces between deep, perennial tide cracks in sea ice.

FOOD

Mainly fish and squid from throughout the water column and on the sea floor under fast ice. Occasionally also penguins. Adults dive on average to 150 metres for 10 minutes per trip, but can reach depths of over 600 metres and spend over 82 minutes under water.

Female Weddell seal and large pup on ice

SOCIAL BEHAVIOUR

The Weddell seal is strongly vocal, producing 21–44 recognisably distinct, complex calls. Males establish underwater territories near their shared breathing holes, defended by almost continuous calling. Females form breeding groups in the same areas.

REPRODUCTION

Males are fertile in October–December. Pups are born on the ice surface in October. Females stay with pups for the first 12 days, then nearby until the end of lactation (6 weeks), losing more than half their body weight while the pup increases from 25-30 kg to 110 kg. Females mate again in the water in December. The delay in implantation is short (1–2 months), so they produce their first pup at 2–6 years old, then annually to around age 18. Males mature at age 3, but do not attend breeding colonies until 5–7 years old, generally unsuccessfully until aged 8–13.

Pups start diving after 2 weeks, and by 6 weeks they can dive to 50–70 metres for 3–4 minutes; by 12 weeks to 100 metres for 5–6 minutes.

POPULATIONS

The annual survival rate of adults is about 80%, but much less (30–60%) in pups and young (ages 0–6). Many Weddell seals were (until 1986) killed to support polar expeditions and for dog meat, but dogs are now banned from Antarctica, and visitors bring their own supplies. A survey in November 2011 of high-resolution satellite images counted about 202,000 Weddell seals around the coasts of Antarctica, not including those that were underwater at the time.

STATUS

DOC Non-resident Vagrant. IUCN Least Concern.

WHERE TO SEE THEM

In the field

Tourist ships can enter the Ross Sea only after January, after seals finish breeding. Vagrants have been recorded on the mainland five times between 1926 and 2007.

In museums

Two mounted Weddell seals are held at Te Papa, and one at the Auckland Museum. Tūhara Otago Museum's Animal Attic has a skull with mandibles.

Leopard seal / popoiangore
Hydrurga leptonyx

IDENTIFICATION

The long, sinuous, well-furred body is built for speed. It is blue-black above, silver below, with large fore-flippers, a large head with a wide gape, and only a few short whiskers. The jaws have long canines and complex, serrated molars.

SIZE

Both sexes average 275–500 kg. Pups are 30 kg at birth.

NEW ZEALAND DISTRIBUTION

Throughout the Ross Dependency. Individuals may be found year-round in New Zealand waters.

HABITAT

On pack ice, and around subantarctic and southern coasts.

FOOD

Krill, fish, penguins, and fur seal pups. Leopard seals frequent the waters surrounding Adélie penguin colonies, catching them after underwater pursuits or those arriving or leaving for the hunt, especially any that slip on the ice. Leopard seals are the only seals that frequently hunt warm-blooded prey, and can impose significant mortality on penguin and fur seal populations. Around New Zealand they also prey upon many small shark species, including elephant fish.

SOCIAL BEHAVIOUR

At least 12 different underwater calls are known, some used during close-range hostile encounters, and some broadcast by receptive females. The

Leopard seal on ice floe

Skin and skeleton of Autahi the leopard seal in Tūhara Otago Museum

lowest frequency call is powerful enough to be audible at the surface and felt through the ice.

REPRODUCTION

Females mature at 2–3 years, and males at 4–6 years. Shifting pack ice prevents the establishment of stable breeding groups monopolised by a dominant male, so competition for mating rights is minimal, and males are not much larger than females. Pups are born on the ice in October–November. First-year mortality is about 25%, but the survivors can live 13–16 years. There are three documented cases of leopard seal pups being born on the coasts of New Zealand.

POPULATIONS

Leopard seals have never been exploited. A population estimate in 1977 put the total number at 222,000–440,000 individuals worldwide, but the proportion of these that live in or visit New Zealand waters is unknown.

STATUS

DOC Naturally uncommon. IUCN Least Concern.

WHERE TO SEE THEM

In the field

Leopard seals may occasionally be seen hauled out on the southern Otago coast, and less regularly further north. One female resident leopard seal named Owha can often be seen around the marinas of Auckland.

In museums

Tūhara Otago Museum's Nature and Otago's Ocean gallery displays the skin and skeleton of a female that died on a local beach in 2009, named Autahi. By negotiation with DOC and iwi, the carcass was sent to be processed into a clean skeleton and skin in matching poses, displayed together with an information board giving her history. Tūhara Otago Museum's Animal Attic has a sagittal section of a skull in a wall case.

Crabeater seal
Lobodon carcinophagus

IDENTIFICATION

The lithe, well-furred body is dark brown above, blond below, and fades to entirely blond with age (they were once called 'white Antarctic seals'). The head is small with only a few short whiskers. The short canines and complex molars fit perfectly together, forming an effective strainer for extracting krill and other small food items from the water.

SIZE

Both sexes average 200 kg as adults, and pups around 30 kg at birth.

NEW ZEALAND DISTRIBUTION

Found throughout the Ross Dependency.

HABITAT

Crabeater seals live mainly on pack ice. Individuals are occasionally found (for unknown reasons) inland on the Antarctic continent, for example in the McMurdo Dry Valleys or on glaciers far from the sea.

FOOD

Their main diet is krill (95%), sieved out of the water through intricately lobed molars. They make over 200 dives per day into the zone where krill is most abundant. These dives are usually short (3 minutes) and shallow (10–40 metres). But they are also capable of much deeper, longer dives of 300–450 metres for at least 15 minutes at a time. One possible explanation is that these deep dives enable crabeater seals to escape surface noise (of ice floes grinding against each other in the swell) to listen for krill swarms. Krill moves closer to the surface at night, so crabeaters prefer to haul out by day and forage at night.

Crabeater seals on ice

SOCIAL BEHAVIOUR

They are unsociable, living alone or in small groups of 2–3. Females with pups are often guarded by a male awaiting his turn. No regular vocal communication is known.

REPRODUCTION

Pups are born on the ice in October, suckle for only 17 days, gain weight at 4 kg/day, and are weaned in November at 80–110 kg.

Females mate again before December, but implantation is delayed for 81 days. Active gestation takes 9 months. Both sexes mature at 6–7 years, and most females pup every year.

POPULATIONS

Crabeater seals are long-lived (more than 10% exceed 20 years; the oldest known was 39 years old) and never seriously exploited. Total population is about 15 million.

STATUS

DOC Non-resident Vagrant. IUCN Least Concern.

WHERE TO SEE THEM

In the field

Individuals have been recorded on the mainland eight times between 1885 and 2015. Five of these were either swimming up the Hutt River or seen on Petone Beach, perhaps diverted from travelling northwards up the east coast of the North Island.

In museums

Six crabeater seals are held in museums: one in the Whanganui Regional Museum, four at Te Papa and one in Canterbury Museum. Tūhara Otago Museum has a skull in the Science Centre, and a full mount in the Animal Attic.

Ross seal
Ommatophoca rossi

IDENTIFICATION

This is the smallest of the Southern Ocean seals. Its graceful body is dark brown above, and silvery below with spots, streaks and very short body hairs. Its generic name (meaning 'eye-seal') derives from its large eyes, with a short snout, small teeth and few whiskers. The fore-flippers have small claws and very long toes.

SIZE

Both sexes average 130–200 kg. Pups are 20 kg at birth.

NEW ZEALAND DISTRIBUTION

Mainly in the Ross Sea, and widely dispersed on circumpolar pack ice.

HABITAT

Ross seals are seldom seen except when breeding or moulting. At other times of the year they spend long periods in open water.

FOOD

Squid, octopus, fish and some krill. One tagged individual averaged 113 dives a day, to all depths from 12 to 400 metres.

SOCIAL BEHAVIOUR

Ross seals are apparently unsociable (most are seen alone, fewer than 10% are seen in pairs), although lone seals are often associated with several others under ice, communicating with each other with loud calls, amplified by resonating chambers in their larynx and a large soft palate.

Head of Ross seal, showing its very large eyes

REPRODUCTION

Pups are born in November. Females re-mate in December, then implantation is delayed till March. Females mature at age 2–4 years, males at 3–4. Both may live around 20 years.

POPULATIONS

They have never been exploited, but are vulnerable to orcas when at sea far from ice. Recent estimates suggest a total population of about 220,000.

STATUS

DOC Non-resident Vagrant. IUCN Least Concern.

WHERE TO SEE THEM

Ross seals are unlikely to be seen unless from a tourist or scientific ship. A single vagrant appeared at Paekākāriki in 2002.

CETACEANS

Introduction

Cetaceans (whales and dolphins) are fully aquatic mammals, superbly specialised to spend their entire lives in water. Whales, dolphins, seals and sea lions are all descended from terrestrial ancestors, but seals and sea lions have to return to land in the breeding season. Cetaceans are the only mammals to have fully adapted to mating, birthing and suckling their young entirely under water. Many of them still retain tiny vestigial hind limbs, visible only in skeletons.

The story of this extraordinary transition is now well documented by a series of amphibious intermediates, preserved as fossils over the last 45 million years. Their history is especially well illustrated by important extinct species found in New Zealand fossil deposits, some of which are on display in our museums.

Fossil history of southern cetaceans

About 35 million years ago, cetaceans began to separate into two quite different lineages. In the Mysticeti (baleen whales), the teeth were lost and replaced by baleen plates suspended from an enlarged upper jaw, an efficient system of filtering swarms of invertebrates out of the water. In the other lineage, the Odontoceti (toothed whales and dolphins), the teeth were retained but simplified into rows of sharp pegs. The two have been evolving separately since about 34 million years ago, and are now very different. Worldwide, there are about 66 species of toothed whales and 10 species of baleen whales, depending on who you ask. The earliest known whales (the Archaeoceti) still showed evidence of their terrestrial origins.

One good example of that transitional stage is seen in the fossil teeth and skull fragments of *Kekenodon onamata*, collected in the Waitaki

Valley, Otago. They belonged to an animal that lived 42.6 million years ago, and had enormous long jaws studded with complex teeth similar to those of land animals. The patterns of wear on these teeth suggest that it had already become an apex marine predator comparable with the modern orca, hunting hard-boned prey such as penguins and other marine mammals.

By 25 million years ago, almost all of Zealandia had sunk below sea level, so much of what is now dry land surrounded by a broad continental shelf was once covered by shallow seas thronging with seabirds, penguins, seals, whales and dolphins. Some of those that died left their skeletons preserved in the accumulated sediments deposited then, until earth movements associated with the building of the Southern Alps lifted their stony graves above the surface.

New Zealand has two magnificent examples of early Odontocetes, represented by important fossils of extinct New Zealand dolphins, both estimated to be about 25–26 million years old. The many species of *Squalodon*, the shark-toothed dolphins, were distributed worldwide as successful near-top predators, but they had to compete with the very large sharks and with other advancing lineages of predatory cetaceans inhabiting the oceans of their time. *Waipatia maerewhenua* was a small archaic dolphin, with skull features showing that it was already capable of echolocation. It represents a new Family, related to but distinct from the *Squalodon* lineages, and is of critical importance in piecing together the evolution of the toothed whales generally.

The evolution of baleen whales was boosted some 30 million years ago by the opening of the Drake Passage (between the southern tip of South America and the Antarctic Peninsula) and the establishment of the circumpolar current roaring clockwise around the Antarctic continent. This, in turn, stimulated huge upwellings of nutrients supporting the algae that grow on the underside of the ice, and the plankton and invertebrate prey that feed on them. Swarms of such small prey, especially

Skull and jaws of extinct dolphin *Squalodon sp.* on display in Tūhura, Otago Museum.

Skull and jaws of extinct dolphin *Waipatia maerewhenu* on display in the University of Otago Geology Museum.

A humpback whale in the Southern Ocean

krill, have made the Southern Ocean a rich feeding ground for cold-adapted cetaceans and penguins for much longer than has the Arctic, which began to freeze less than 5 million years ago. The evolution of huge baleen whales has been continuing in their 'cold southern cradle' for at least 20 million years.

The New Zealand fossil record supplies an early example of this stage too. The Dawn Baleen Whale *Tokarahia kauaeroa*, which is 26 million years old, was found in the Otekaieke limestone deposits in Otago.

WHERE TO SEE THEM

The geology of the Waitaki Valley, North Otago, has long been recognised as a unique location for studies of New Zealand fossil history. A generally flat tableland, it is underlain by thick slabs of horizontal limestone, dissected by rivers into valleys bounded by steep cliffs, most with scattered detached blocks and boulders at their feet. Embedded in the limestone and exposed by erosion, some 13 species of fossil whales of

Oligocene age have been recovered from the Waitaki area alone.

The sequence of richly fossiliferous rocks exposed in the limestone escarpments of the Waitaki Valley, and its many other significant geological features, is so important that the entire area has been recognised as New Zealand's first UNESCO Global Geopark, the Waitaki Whitestone Geopark. In the middle of the geopark is the village of Duntroon, and the Vanished World Centre. Casts of all the fossils listed above can be seen in the centre's museum, along with informative displays, models and paintings, and there is a guide to a self-drive tour around some of the sites where fossils have been found. The original fossils are held in Tūhara Otago Museum or the University of Otago's Geology Museum. Te Papa also has a cast of the shark-toothed dolphin skull in its Te Taiao | Nature gallery.

LIVING CETACEANS

Table 2 lists the total number of cetacean species recognised by DOC in 2019 as members of the native mammal fauna of New Zealand. Almost half of the known cetacean species worldwide are recorded from the New Zealand Region, but in this book we describe only a selection of living species that might be seen from shore, or from whale watching vessels in our coastal waters, or in Antarctica, or have been stranded, or are significant to New Zealand whaling history. The great majority are classed as Data Deficient or Not Threatened, leaving only three as Nationally Critical, one as Nationally Endangered and one as Nationally Vulnerable. Only the two subspecies of the New Zealand dolphin *Cephalorhynchus hectori* are at serious risk of extinction.

The living Odontocetes (toothed whales) include dolphins, sperm whales, beaked whales and porpoises. They are all fast swimmers, actively hunting fish and squid, often diving to great depths. They all have single blow-holes, and range in size from the 1.4-metre New Zealand dolphins (small by cetacean standards) to the 16-metre-or-longer sperm

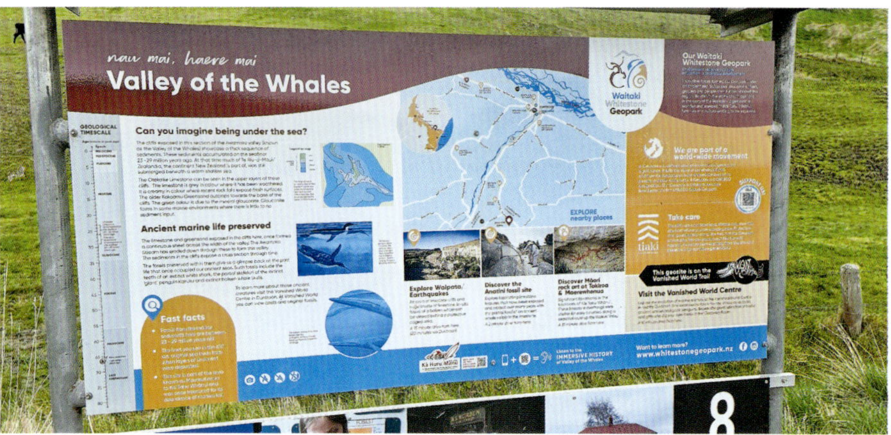

Valley of the Whales and its information board near Duntroon

whale. The earliest species were known only from isolated teeth until the first full skulls were found.

Odontocetes use echolocation, emitting a variety of clicks generated by their single blowhole to create a stream of sound signals for communication and navigation. They have large brains in relation to their body mass, and a 'melon' in the head, used to focus sound waves. Some have more than 100 simple peg-like teeth, and others have only a few more bizarrely shaped teeth, more for display than for hunting.

By contrast, the Mysticetes (baleen whales) have no teeth, but their gigantic upper jaws are hung with fringed baleen plates made of keratin. They swim slowly near the surface, searching the wind for the scent of aggregations of krill when coming up for air. Then, when finding one, they can take in huge volumes of water into their expandable mouths. They use their massive tongue to force water out sideways past the baleen plates that strain out small food items. This filtering system is very efficient, and allows the baleen whales to reach enormous sizes. Eight of the 14 known species have been sighted in New Zealand waters.

ODONTOCETES / TOOTHED WHALES AND DOLPHINS

Dolphins

The most familiar of the toothed whales are the dolphins, a worldwide group of 38 species of small (most less than 4 metres long), agile, fast-swimming cetaceans with slender, streamlined bodies, large dorsal fins and pointed snouts. Some 18 species are known in New Zealand waters.

South Island New Zealand dolphin / Hector's dolphin / tutumairekurai / tūpoupou / pahu
Cephalorhynchus hectori hectori

IDENTIFICATION

The body is rotund, the head pointed with no beak, grey on the back with black cheeks and snout, pale grey to white on the cap, and white on the throat and belly, black flippers and under tail and flukes. The dorsal fin and flippers are smoothly rounded. The jaws have 27–32 pairs of teeth.

The species name *hectori* was given when these dolphins were first formally described in 1881, to honour one of New Zealand's premier early scientists, Sir James Hector. Hence, the former common name of 'Hector's dolphin'. More recently, that colonial-era tag has been dropped in order to recognise this dolphin's unique status as resident only in New Zealand.

SIZE

Adults average 1.4 metres long, and can weigh up to 50 kg. They are the smallest dolphins of the family. Females average slightly larger than males.

NEW ZEALAND DISTRIBUTION

Close to shore and in estuaries all around South Island coasts. These small dolphins are attracted to set nets, and are very vulnerable to entanglement in them.

FOOD

Shallow water/bottom-living fish, cuttlefish, shrimps, crustaceans. They feed even in silty water near estuaries, hunting by echolocation during short, not deep dives.

SOCIAL BEHAVIOUR

The South Island New Zealand dolphin lives in small, sociable groups of 2–10. They are very friendly to small boats and swimmers.

POPULATIONS

The populations of the South Island New Zealand dolphin on the east, west and northwest coasts of South Island are genetically distinct from each other, and total about 15,000 individuals over a year old.

Females can birth a calf only every 2–4 years, which will stay with its mother for up to two years. That means that, although undisturbed females can live up to 25 years, they may not be able to produce more than 5–6 calves in their lifetime.

In the 1980s, at least 230 South Island New Zealand dolphins had been recorded drowned in gill nets off the Canterbury coast over only four years, out of a population then estimated at about 740. The immediate result was the establishment in December 1988 of New Zealand's first marine sanctuary of 1,170 km². In October 2008, three new sanctuaries were declared especially for New Zealand dolphins, where set netting and trawling are limited or prohibited, but the total numbers are still declining. Gill nets are especially dangerous because dolphins cannot swim backwards to avoid becoming entangled.

New Zealand South Island dolphin (Hector's dolphin) and calf, Akaroa Harbour

STATUS

DOC Nationally Vulnerable. IUCN Endangered.

WHERE TO SEE THEM

In the field

Dolphin watching companies advertise their current schedules on the internet. Curio Bay in the Catlins is a reliable viewing location, used by about 20 dolphins as a nursery area.

In museums

Te Papa's Te Taiao | Nature gallery has a skull. Tūhara Otago Museum's Animal Attic has a mostly complete articulated skeleton in a wall case.

North Island New Zealand dolphin / Māui's dolphin / popoto
Cephalorhynchus hectori maui

IDENTIFICATION

Māui's dolphin is a genetically and geographically distinct subspecies of the New Zealand dolphin, always resident off the west of the North Island, never visiting the South Island. Its southern equivalent, the South Island New Zealand dolphin, is never found in the waters around the North Island. The two look and behave almost the same, and both are unmistakable, because no other dolphins have a rounded dorsal fin.

NEW ZEALAND DISTRIBUTION

Close to shore and in estuaries along west coast of the North Island, from Kaipara Harbour south to New Plymouth. They are most often seen in shallow waters (less than 100 metres deep) within a few kilometres of the coast between Manukau Harbour and Raglan.

POPULATIONS

The geographical and reproductive separation of the two subspecies must have been continuous for a very long time, at least 15,000 years. Māui's dolphins probably once numbered in the thousands, but now only about 55 adults (more than 1 year old) are left, of which maybe 14–20 are breeding females aged over 7–9 years old. Females do not reach breeding age until then, and after that have only one calf every 2–4 years. Hence the potential recovery rate of the only remaining population is extremely slow, and they cannot withstand any accidental mortality in fishing nets.

Drowned dolphins tangled in netting

STATUS

DOC Nationally Critical. IUCN Not Assessed.

WHERE TO SEE THEM

In the field

A marine mammal sanctuary to cover Māui's entire distribution, from Maunganui Bluff in Northland to Ōakura Beach in Taranaki, in all waters less than 100 m deep, was established in October 2008. Set netting is banned within 7 nautical miles of the coast, and trawling within 2 nautical miles of the coast. In addition, all set netting is banned in the Manukau Harbour entrance west of Puponga Point (Cornwallis) to 0.5 nautical miles north of Kauri Point (at the eastern end of Big Bay).

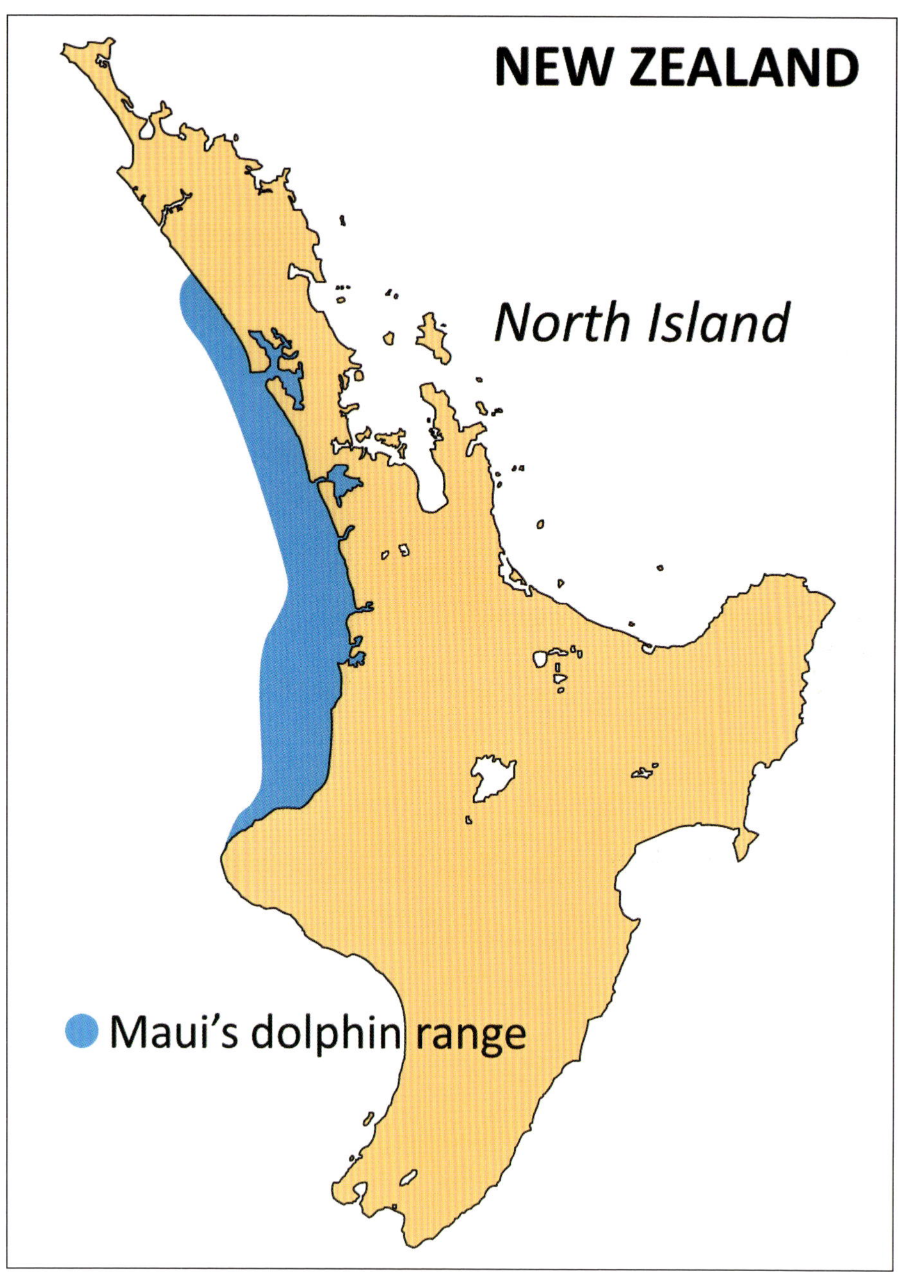

Distribution of Māui's dolphin

Risso's dolphin
Grampus griseus

IDENTIFICATION
The body is grey above, paler below, fading to almost white with age, and invariably with multiple pale scars especially forward of the dorsal fin. The head is blunt and bulbous with a deep median crease. The flippers are long and pointed, and the dorsal fin tall (50 cm) and straight. The 4–14 teeth are set only at front end of the lower jaw, and there are usually none (but sometimes 1-2 pairs) in the upper jaw. In older adults, some or all of the teeth may be worn-down or missing.

SIZE
Adults average 3 metres, and 300 kg. Calves are 1.5 metres at birth.

NEW ZEALAND DISTRIBUTION
Risso's dolphins are mostly tropical, so are uncommon in New Zealand. But 'Pelorus Jack', one of the most famous dolphins in New Zealand history, belonged to this species. Between 1888 and 1912, Jack regularly rode the bow waves of steamers passing the entrance of Pelorus Sound, accompanying them to Admiralty Bay. He even had his own protection order under the Sea-fisheries Act 1894, as a named individual not a fish, signed by the New Zealand Colonial Governor in 1904 (he was too early to be included under the Marine Mammals Protection act of 1978). By the time he disappeared in 1912, his size (around 3.7 metres, near maximum), and colour (pale to white) confirmed his age as at least 34, a good record for a dolphin.

FOOD
Mainly squid, especially at night when deep-water squid tend to rise closer to the surface.

Risso's dolphin

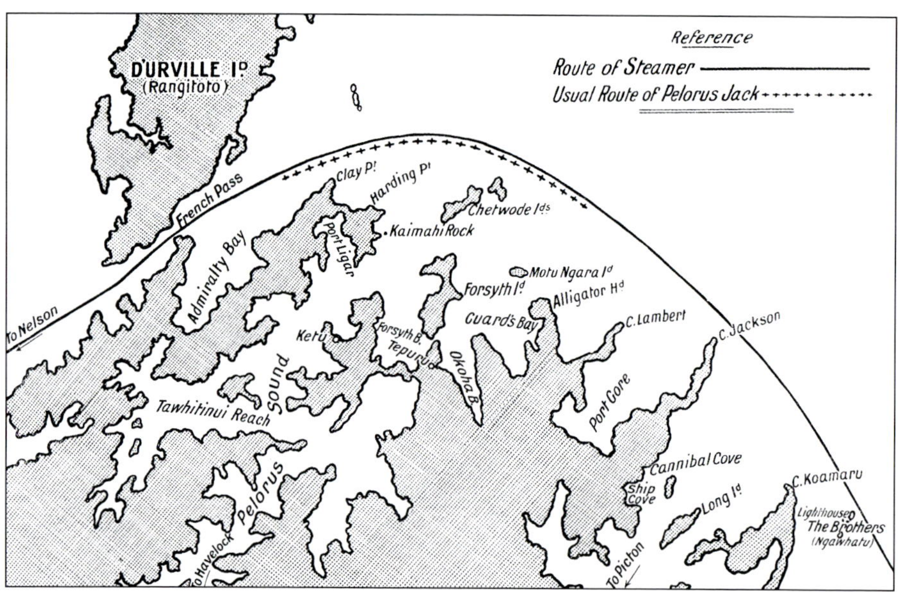

Map of Pelorus Jack's regular route accompanying steamers sailing between Wellington (at right) to Nelson across the northern entrance to Pelorus Sound.

REPRODUCTION

Gestation takes 13–14 months, and calves may appear any time of year.

POPULATIONS

Abundant globally, living in social groups of 3–30, especially in warmer waters. There are few stranding records. One group of six was found inside Whangārei Harbour in 1983. Four stranded and two were guided back to sea, but within a week they returned, and all died.

STATUS

DOC See Table 2. IUCN Least Concern

WHERE TO SEE THEM

Sightings in New Zealand waters are very rare.

Bottlenose dolphin / terehu
Tursiops truncatus

IDENTIFICATION

The body is light grey, shading to pinkish white, with a tall, dark dorsal fin. The short strong beak has 18–27 pairs of large (6 mm diameter) teeth in both jaws. The lower jaw protrudes beyond the upper, and the corner of mouth curves upwards in a permanent 'grin'. Bottlenose dolphins are very athletic, and seem to enjoy jumping out of the water. They are friendly and often willing to approach boats and cooperate with people.

SIZE

Adults are 2–4 metres, and 200 kg. Calves are 1 metre and 32 kg at birth.

Bottlenose dolphins jumping

NEW ZEALAND DISTRIBUTION

The three independent subpopulations (one in the North Island, one in Marlborough Sounds, and one in Fiordland) are isolated from each other. The northern group is common near shore between Tauranga and Doubtless Bay, usually seen in small groups of up to 30.

FOOD

The broad diet of bottlenose dolphins includes any inshore bottom-dwelling fish or crabs. They may follow trawlers for discards, or hunt in cooperative packs. Some have been observed to kill fish by whacking them with their tails, or working together to push shoals out onto mudflats, at the risk of stranding themselves, to collect their helpless prey.

SOCIAL BEHAVIOUR

Bottlenose dolphins are very gregarious, willingly associating with their own and other cetacean species. They are quick to learn, can be accurate mimics of other animals, and seem to enjoy human company, so are easily studied.

The famous 'Opo' was a young female bottlenose dolphin who regularly mingled with swimmers at Opononi in the summer of 1955–56. She attracted crowds of visitors, especially many fascinated children, and a great deal of publicity that benefited the local tourist industry. A special effort to protect her was made in the form of the Fisheries (Dolphin Protection) Regulations 1956, issued on 7 March 1956 and notified in the *New Zealand Gazette* on 8 March. Sadly, Opo died, probably on the same day. A memorial to her now stands outside the local pub.

In January 2010, a male bottlenose dolphin visited Whakatāne. 'Moko' was often seen around Whakatāne, at Ōhope Beach, where he joined in with the surfers at West End, and in Otarawairere Bay where he swam with locals up the Whakatāne River. He was found dead on Matakana Island in June 2010.

Some bottlenose dolphins have been trained for military purposes,

Opo the celebrity dolphin entertains visitors in 1956

such as to search for mines on the sea floor. They are the species most commonly believed to come to the rescue of humans in trouble at sea, or even of other cetaceans.

REPRODUCTION

Courtship behaviour is elaborate. Cooperative actions and complex communication suggest high intelligence. Females mature at between 5 and 13 years, males slightly later. They can live into their forties or early fifties.

Gestation is 12 months, and births are attended by 'midwives', who wait as the calf emerges tail first and carry it to the surface to breathe. Lactation lasts a year. Calving intervals average two years, so females can expect to produce only about eight calves in a lifetime. Calf mortality from propeller strikes is high in areas with many tourist boats.

POPULATIONS

Globally common, but not in New Zealand. Around 450 individuals live in the northern North Island, where there are currently (2020) some 26 individual dolphins visiting the Bay of Islands. Around 63 live in Doubtful Sound, Fiordland. The number living in the group ranging from the Marlborough Sounds to Westport is unknown.

STATUS

DOC Nationally Endangered; the Fiordland subpopulation is classed as Critically Endangered, confined to a special Protection Zone. IUCN Least Concern.

WHERE TO SEE THEM

In the field

Sighting wild bottlenose dolphins is the main objective of dolphin watching cruises in harbours north of Hauraki Gulf, where they are natural acrobats and bow-wave riders.

In museums

Te Papa's Te Taiao | Nature gallery and Tūhura Otago Museum's Science Centre of both have a skull on display.

Dusky dolphin
Lagenorhynchus obscurus

IDENTIFICATION

The blue-black skin on the back is crossed by broad white stripes down to the tail. The underside is white, the snout dark with almost no beak, and the flippers grey. The dorsal fin is dark in front, and the trailing edge is grey. The jaws have 27–36 pairs of small (3 mm diameter) teeth.

SIZE

Adults are 1.6–1.8 metres, and 115 kg. Calves are 90 cm and 5 kg at birth.

NEW ZEALAND DISTRIBUTION

Common in the cooler temperate waters from Hawke's Bay south to Oamaru and east to the Chatham Islands. Rare elsewhere. In 1977, three dusky dolphins were reported as stranded on Campbell Island.

FOOD

Fish, squid and various bottom-dwelling prey. In some places, like Kaikōura, they feed mainly at night, when benthic species migrate vertically from deep water to nearer the surface.

SOCIAL BEHAVIOUR

Dusky dolphins are spectacular natural acrobats, leaping and somersaulting spontaneously at sea. When one starts, many others follow. They are also capable of bow-riding vessels moving at 35kph, especially small boats.

REPRODUCTION

Dusky dolphins are social and gregarious, swimming in groups with their own and other species. Casual sexual behaviour can be observed at any time, but mating leading to pregnancy is most common in summer or

A dusky dolphin off the coast of Kaikōura

early autumn. Gestation takes about 9 months, and most calves appear from late October to mid-January.

POPULATION

Between 12,000 and 20,000 in New Zealand, but they are vulnerable to drowning in gill nets and purse seines.

STATUS

DOC See Table 2. IUCN category Data Deficient.

WHERE TO SEE THEM

In the field

Dusky dolphins are often seen from whale watching vessels off Kaikōura.

In museums

Te Papa's Te Taiao | Nature gallery has a skull. Auckland Museum's Weird & Wonderful Discovery Centre, and Tūhara Otago Museum's Nature and Otago's Ocean gallery, both have fibreglass models of dusky dolphins.

Long-finned pilot whale / blackfish/ upokohue
Globicephala melas

IDENTIFICATION

The large bulbous head (source of its Latin name, meaning 'globe-head') has a blunt nose and an upward-sloping mouth with 8–13 pairs of teeth in each jaw. The body is black (hence the alternative name of 'blackfish'), except for a saddle of white behind the dorsal fin and patches of pinkish-grey forward of the flippers, extending as a thin band along the midline of the mainly grey belly. The dorsal fin is steeply curved, and broad at the base. The flippers are long (18–27% of body length) and sickle-shaped.

SIZE

Adults are 5–7 metres, and 1.3–4 tonnes. Calves are 1.8 metres and 100 kg at birth.

NEW ZEALAND DISTRIBUTION

Long-finned pilot whales are common around the New Zealand coast, foraging in deeper, cooler waters well offshore.

FOOD

Squid and fish. Most dives reach only to 30–60 metres, but they can easily go much deeper, even to 1,000 metres.

SOCIAL BEHAVIOUR

Social cohesion is extremely strong, maintained by a continuous stream of varied sound signals, so whatever happens to any one of a large group usually affects them all. Travelling groups move in line astern or along a broad front, with mature males leading. At sea, groups are relatively stable, hierarchical and polygamous, and families sleep in close contact.

This strong social bonding makes them vulnerable to strandings, which usually include large groups. In one study of 120 mass strandings, the average group size was 78, but several were 200+. Some of these could have been short-finned pilot whales, recognised as a separate species only in 1977. Strandings of such large groups are often dramatic, since surviving or refloated individuals will not leave beached pod-mates while they are still alive. In New Zealand alone, more than 10,000 pilot whales have stranded in the last 100 years, including one group of around 1,000 beached on Chatham Island in 1918, and 450 on Great Barrier Island in 1985.

REPRODUCTION

Both sexes mature at around 6 years. Females can breed from then until their thirties, but males not until they reach about 12 years. Gestation is 16 months, and births can be recorded in all seasons. Lactation lasts around 20 months.

STATUS

DOC See Table 2. IUCN Least Concern.

WHERE TO SEE THEM

Te Papa's Te Taiao | Nature gallery displays a skull. For responses to strandings, see page 19.

Long-finned pilot whale

Short-beaked common dolphin / aihe
Delphinus delphis

IDENTIFICATION

The body is dark above, pale below, with a distinct 'hourglass' colour pattern on the flanks and a tall dark dorsal fin. A pale frontal stripe crosses the otherwise dark head above a black eye spot and black beak, and a dark stripe crosses the white area below the chin. The flippers are dark to grey. There are 41–57 pairs of small (3 mm diameter) teeth in the upper and lower jaws.

SIZE

Adults average 2 metres and normally weigh 80-150 kg. Calves are 90 cm at birth.

NEW ZEALAND DISTRIBUTION

Common in coastal waters all round New Zealand, these dolphins are often seen travelling in large pods of over 200 together. Groups are naturally playful, often seen bow-riding regardless of boat speed, rolling sideways to squint up at humans, and whistling to each other loud enough for boat passengers to hear.

Strandings of single animals are often recorded, but few in large groups. They are vulnerable to drowning as by-catch in the trawl fishery (115 killed over 10 years 1998–2008, plus another 24 entangled in nets).

FOOD

Squid, schooling fish (sardines, anchovy) and crabs.

SOCIAL BEHAVIOUR

Groups commonly numbering 20–200+, even thousands, are segregated by age and sex, each with an internal dominance hierarchy. Group members practice remarkable but well-documented mutual assistance

Common dolphin

(supporting injured individuals, and cooperative hunting or defence against sharks). They often forage in mixed-species groups with other dolphins and seabirds, and may practice cooperative herding of fish schools against the water surface.

REPRODUCTION

Gestation is 10–11 months, and calves are nursed for at least 12 months. Females mature at between 5 and 13 years of age, then can produce calves every second year. Both sexes can live till at least 25 years old.

POPULATION

About 6,000,000 globally.

STATUS

DOC See Table 2. IUCN Least Concern.

WHERE TO SEE THEM

In the field

Three regional sub populations live in the coastal waters around New Zealand, all isolated from each other and from a fourth pelagic group that ranges further from land. A North Island sub population lives mainly in the Bay of Islands, and numbers at least 400 known individuals. Another sub population comprising more than 380 dolphins regularly visits the Marlborough Sounds, including 335 identified as individuals (1992-2005 data). The third regional subpopulation is much smaller, and split into three local units of around 50-100 members each.

In museums

Auckland Museum's Weird & Wonderful Discovery Centre has a skeleton and a full-body model of a common dolphin.

Orca / killer whale / kākahi / maki / kera wēra
Orcinus orca

IDENTIFICATION

The body has bold, unmistakable, black and white markings, individually variable. The blunt, powerful head has 10–14 pairs of large conical teeth in each jaw, oval in section. The flippers are large and rounded. The tall dorsal fin of males is straight and reaches to 1.9 metres, contrasting with the female's slightly hooked and shorter dorsal fin at 0.9 metres. The grey saddle patch behind the dorsal fin is individually unique. Weights of 7–10 tonnes make these by far the largest members of the dolphin family. The common name was originally 'whale killers', given by whalers observing them attacking other cetaceans, but was later changed to 'killer whales', a pejorative term now dropped in favour of the more correct and neutral name 'orca'.

SIZE

Males measure 8–9 metres, and weigh up to 10 tonnes. Females are 7–8 metres in length and weigh 7.5 tonnes. Calves average around 2–2.5 metres, and are 160–180 kg at birth.

NEW ZEALAND DISTRIBUTION

Orcas are commonly seen in New Zealand coastal waters, even inside enclosed areas, including Wellington Harbour and in the Bay of Islands, but they are very mobile so frequent sightings do not necessarily equate to more than a few hundred individuals in fast-moving groups. Mass strandings are rare (the largest known was 17 at Paraparaumu in 1955, and 11 on Chatham Island in 1981).

FOOD

Most dives are short and shallow, but hunting is strongly cooperative.

Orca swimming under water

Orca blowing

They are fast and powerful swimmers and have developed such efficient pack-hunting methods that few chosen prey can escape. Prey includes almost anything they can handle: fish, squid, rays, sharks, seals, sea lions, seabirds, small dolphins and young baleen whales. Orca were once believed to be dangerously aggressive (one early name meant 'demon dolphin') but no deliberate fatal attacks on humans have ever been recorded.

SOCIAL BEHAVIOUR

Strongly social, coordinating their activities with complex calls. Extended family pods include young of both sexes and all ages staying with their mother for life, an unusual trait among cetaceans. Pods are usually 2–40 strong.

REPRODUCTION

Females can produce their first calf at age 12–15 years, and thereafter on average one every five years or so until their forties, for a lifetime total of five calves. Gestation takes 15-18 months, and weaning starts after about one year, but lactation can continue for two. Calves are born in shallow water in autumn/early winter.

POPULATIONS

The Southern Ocean population comes in four distinct types: A, B, C and D. Most orca in New Zealand are of the A type, and live in three distinguishable sub populations — one each in North and South Island waters and a third more mobile. The total resident population in New Zealand is estimated at between 150 and 200, of which at least 117 individuals are identified and named. The taxonomic status of these subgroups is still undetermined.

STATUS

DOC Nationally Critical. IUCN Data Deficient. IUCN's ranking is due to uncertainty over the taxonomic status of the separate sub populations. If these are recognised as separate species, the IUCN ranking would change.

WHERE TO SEE THEM

In museums

Auckland Museum's Weird & Wonderful Discovery Centre and Tūhara Otago Museum's Nature and Otago's Ocean gallery both have orca skulls.

False killer whale
Pseudorca crassidens

IDENTIFICATION

The slim body is entirely black, except for a grey patch on the throat and chest. The rounded snout has 7–12 pairs of large teeth in both upper and lower jaws, circular in section. The flippers are slightly curved on the leading edge, and the dorsal fin is sharply raked. These dolphins are fast-swimming for their size, and are the largest cetaceans capable of bow-wave riding, but are not fast enough to enjoy it if the ship is doing more than 25 km/h. The name is based on similarities with orca in the structure of the skull and teeth, otherwise the two do not look much alike.

SIZE

Adults measure 4–6 metres and weigh 1-2 tonnes. Calves are 1.5 metres and 80 kg at birth.

NEW ZEALAND DISTRIBUTION

The habitat of the false killer whale is deep coastal and offshore waters, especially in warmer areas around the eastern North Island and the Chatham Islands.

FOOD

Squid and fish, including fast-swimming species such as bonito, swordfish and tuna. They are not shy about approaching boats, and have been known to raid long-lines for fish.

SOCIAL BEHAVIOUR

False killer whales travel in pods hundreds strong, leading to some very large mass strandings (231 at Manukau in 1978). Pod members often breach, and communicate with each other by diverse, piercing whistles audible to humans.

A large pod of false killer whales

REPRODUCTION

Adults mature at 8–12 years, and breed any time of year. Gestation takes 15 months, and lactation two years.

STATUS

DOC See Table 2. IUCN Data Deficient

Southern right whale dolphin
Lissodelphis peronii

IDENTIFICATION

The body is sleek and slender, black on the back and tail, contrasting with the white snout, throat, flippers, belly and underside of flukes. There are 40–49 pairs of small pointed teeth in both upper and lower jaws. They are named after the southern right whale (page 127) because it also has no dorsal fin. Instead, the body is flattened with flippers placed at the extreme widest point, which is enough to maintain stability.

SIZE

Adults average up to 3 metres, and weigh up to 116 kg.

NEW ZEALAND DISTRIBUTION

These dolphins usually stay in cool, deep waters well offshore, but can occasionally be seen off the South Island and Chatham Islands. They feed on fish and squid in groups of up to 1,000. Strandings are not common, but 75 of them were beached together on the Chatham Islands in 1988. The New Zealand population is unknown.

STATUS

DOC See Table 2. IUCN Data Deficient.

Southern right whale dolphin, showing the lack of a dorsal fin

Short-finned pilot whale
Globiocephala macrorhynchus

IDENTIFICATION

Similar in general appearance to its long-finned relative, but smaller, with a pale grey saddle, grey streaks behind the eye, shorter flippers (less than 18% of its body length) and fewer teeth (7–9 pairs in each jaw).

SIZE

Adults measure 4–7 metres and weigh 1.5–3 tonnes. Calves are less than 1.5 metres and are 60 kg at birth.

NEW ZEALAND DISTRIBUTION

Mostly tropical, preferring waters of at least 22°C, so they are seldom seen around the New Zealand coast, and then only off the northern North Island. Still, at least seven mass strandings (127 animals) since 1977 were definitely this species. There might have been more, but previously this species was not distinguished from the long-finned pilot whale.

Short-finned pilot whale

FOOD

Squid, including deep-water species, for which short-finned pilot whales can dive up to 800 metres. Unfamiliarity with shallow water may be the cause of confusion leading to mass strandings.

REPRODUCTION

Mature females and their female calves remain together for life, including a long nursing period extended into years for the last calf. Young males disperse, visiting female-dominated pods in search of mates.

STATUS

DOC See Table 2. IUCN Data Deficient.

ODONTOCETES /SPERM WHALES and BEAKED WHALES

This group includes the largest and most famous of all toothed whales, the central character of Melville's book *Moby Dick*. Sperm whales all have a spermaceti organ, no visible teeth in the upper jaw, and use echolocation for hunting and social communication. The family name comes from the (wrong) idea by early whalers that the spermaceti organ (a reservoir of clear liquid that sets to solid wax on cooling) was connected with reproduction.

Less known are the beaked whales. Not all of the thirteen species known to visit New Zealand are mentioned here. All are medium sized, with a pointed beak and few teeth, living in deep water far offshore. Most are very difficult to tell apart, and typically seen only as strandings, which are uncommon.

Sperm whale / parāoa / pāmu wēra
Physeter macrocephalus

IDENTIFICATION

The body is grey, covered with a corrugated hide showing a few white patches that become larger with age. Occasionally, white individuals with albinism or leucism are spotted, but they are extremely rare. The huge square head (occupying 35% of the body length) has a relatively small terminal blowhole on the front left side. The blow therefore angles distinctly forward and leftwards. The brain is huge, up to 8 kg, and the spermaceti organ can hold up to 25,000 kg of oil used for buoyancy and echolocation. The 18–26 pairs of teeth measure 20 cm long and 10 cm in diameter, with no enamel. The teeth appear only after age 10, and in the underslung lower jaw only, because the teeth of the upper jaw seldom erupt. There is no true dorsal fin, but a series of low humps or ridges along the spine. The flippers are small relative to the size of the body. Clean skeletons reveal small pelvic girdles buried under the skin. The very broad flukes are dark underneath, and always show on diving.

SIZE

Adults average 11–16 metres, and weigh 15–50 tonnes (males are more than twice as large as females). Calves are 4 metres, 1000-1500 kg at birth.

NEW ZEALAND DISTRIBUTION

Females and calves are mostly confined to warm subtropical waters. Males travel south to the colder high latitudes in summer to feed, alone or in casual bachelor herds, returning north in winter.

FOOD

Adults specialise on deep-water squid, and frequently dive to below 1,000 metres to find them. Their gullet is the largest of any cetacean, permitting

A sperm whale dives straight down, lifting its flukes as it leaves the surface

The sperm whale has teeth only in its underslung lower jaw

them to swallow even giant squid in one piece. They lift their flukes clear of the surface when diving straight down, staying down for more than two hours. The head and jaws of most adult sperm whales are patterned with circular scars up to 12–15 cm diameter, made by the suckers on squid tentacles. Other food items include sharks up to 4 metres long, skates and fish. During deep dives, cold water cools the spermaceti organ and increases its density, providing neutral buoyancy at any depth.

SOCIAL BEHAVIOUR

Sperm whale society is complex. Males over 25 years old are mostly solitary, except when visiting nursery pods for mating in winter. They are not aggressive, but, if rammed accidentally while sleeping at the surface, they have been known to turn and attack even a large ship. Females and calves live in large, stable, strongly bonded pods, nursing for 2–3 years their own and each other's calves. They keep in contact by echolocation, with each producing individually distinct clicks. Young males join bachelor groups until they are old enough to breed at 20–25 years old, congregating at feeding grounds such as at Kaikōura.

Mass strandings (usually females and calves) were recorded near Gisborne in 1970 (59 whales) and at Muriwai in 1974 (72 whales) and three later occasions. These events seem to be initiated by a single beached individual whose distress calls bring the others in. The rest of the pod can be prevented from stranding only if the injured animal is quickly silenced. Males are less strongly bonded, so less likely to strand together.

REPRODUCTION

Gestation takes 14–16 months, and lactation 12–24 months. Then follows a resting phase of 9 months, so the entire breeding cycle can be 5 years. Females help each other to breathe while giving birth, and to defend calves from attack by orca.

POPULATIONS

During the nineteenth and twentieth centuries, whalers took advantage of the social bonding among sperm whales to kill tens of thousands a year. The present total population is probably no more than 380,000, of which 60–100 visit New Zealand waters, but ocean pollution is now potentially a much worse threat. Gut contents sometimes record boots, buckets and plastic bags, and cast whales often die with their guts blocked with plastic. Plastic debris and lengths of mussel spat rope have been found covered in ambergris, showing that it counteracts irritants in the gut. The gradual decline in the number of sperm whales visiting Kaikōura since 2007, at least during summer but not winter, is perhaps linked to the rise in global sea-surface temperatures and the spread of ocean pollution.

STATUS

DOC See Table 2. IUCN Vulnerable.

WHERE TO SEE THEM

In the field

Sperm whales are still common enough around Cook Strait to support commercial whale watching trips from Kaikōura.

In museums

The natural size and position of the sperm whale's teeth can be appreciated from the full lower jaw displayed at human eye level in Auckland Museum's Imaginarium gallery. Tūhara Otago Museum has a single sperm whale lower jaw suspended from the ceiling of the entrance hall, and a complete mandible including the teeth in the Southern Land, Southern People gallery. There is a beautifully carved tooth on display in Te Papa's Te Taiao | Nature gallery from a sperm whale stranded in 1995, carved by Rangi Kip (Taranaki Te Āti Awa) and purchased by Te Papa in 2018.

Pygmy sperm whale
Kogia breviceps

IDENTIFICATION

The body is short at 3–3.5 metres, and is grey, even purplish, on the back, and whitish to pinkish below, seldom scarred. It has a curved dorsal fin, short broad flippers, a white bracket mark ('false gill') behind the eye, and a white spot forward of the eye. The blunt head has a bulbous nose filled with spermaceti, comprising about 15% of the body. The blowhole is on the top left of the head, and the blow is inconspicuous. There are 12–16 pairs of recurved, sharp teeth in the lower jaw.

SIZE

Adults average 3 metres and weigh 400 kg. Calves are 1 metre and 55 kg at birth.

Pygmy Sperm Whale

NEW ZEALAND DISTRIBUTION

Pygmy sperm whales are rarely seen at sea, but often strand on the New Zealand coast (more than 300 known cases), especially off the Māhia Peninsula, usually alone or in mother–calf pairs. In 2008, well-known bottlenose dolphin 'Moko' (page 91) found two stranded pygmy sperm whales on Māhia Beach, and led them back to open water.

POPULATIONS

Their numbers are not known. Between dives they tend to lie on the surface, where they are hard to spot and vulnerable to boat strikes.

STATUS

DOC See Table 2. IUCN Data Deficient.

Gray's beaked whale / hakurā / iheih
Mesoplodon grayi

IDENTIFICATION

The slender body is deep grey to black, paler grey below, with paler spots and scars scattered throughout. The jaws and throat are white. There is a small dorsal fin and short, wide flippers. Both sexes have only one pair of triangular, laterally flattened, pointed teeth on the lower jaw, while the upper jaw contains only 17–22 smaller teeth. The head has a small bulge in front of the blowhole, and two prominent throat grooves.

SIZE

Adults measure 3–4 metres, and around 1 tonne.

NEW ZEALAND DISTRIBUTION

Gray's beaked whale is a sociable southern hemisphere species best known from strandings in New Zealand. The species was first discovered after 28 of them stranded on Chatham Island in 1874, and

An unidentified beaked whale stranded near Whangarei

there have been another 180 cases since, especially on the northern coast of the North Island. The large number of standings of mothers with dependent young suggests that females move closer to the shore during the summer calving season.

STATUS

DOC See Table 2. IUCN Data Deficient.

WHERE TO SEE THEM

Te Papa's Te Taiao | Nature gallery has a skull. Auckland Museum's Origins gallery has a worn mandible of an unidentified species of beaked whale, *Mesoplodon sp.*, dredged up from the sea floor off the South Island, similar to fossils 8–12 million years old known from the same area.

Strap-toothed whale
Mesoplodon layardii

IDENTIFICATION

The long body is laterally compressed, dark grey underneath, paler above, with a large white patch on top of the head and throat, and around the vent. The long, slender beak is mostly white, but the top of the head and around the eye remain dark. The flippers and dorsal fin are small. Males have a single pair of large, strap-shaped teeth (30 cm long, 4–5 cm wide) protruding backwards at a 45 degrees angle from the lower jaw, curving over the upper jaw, which can eventually limit the opening of the mouth. The teeth of females never erupt.

FOOD

They appear to feed by sucking in small squid and fish. They often bask at the surface of calm waters, and when diving they sink slowly without raising their tail. They are shy of boats, so when spotted they can disappear with hardly a ripple. They are not strongly sociable.

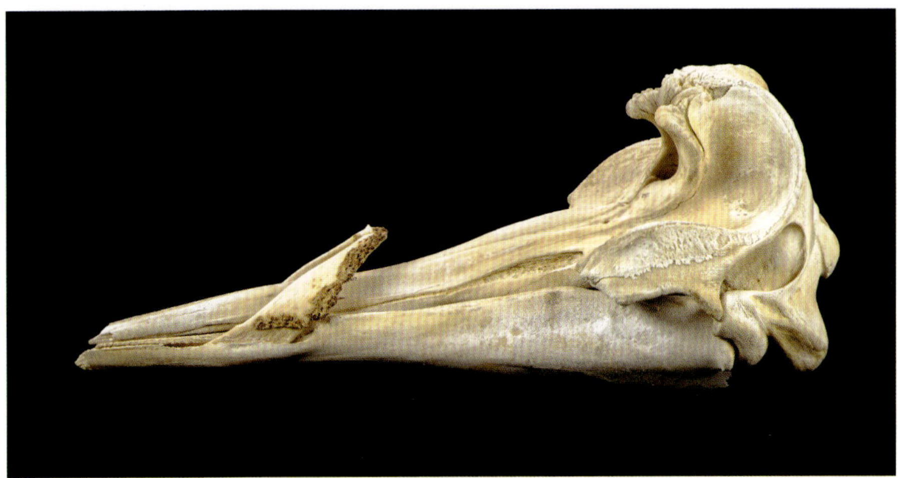

Skull of a strap-toothed whale on display in Te Papa's Te Taiao | Nature gallery.

SIZE

Adults measure 5–7 metres, and around 1–2 tonnes.

NEW ZEALAND DISTRIBUTION

Restricted to the southern hemisphere, where this species is common and tends to move closer to the New Zealand coast in summer. Small groups of 2–3 often strand off the northern North Island between January and April.

STATUS

DOC, IUCN, both Data Deficient

WHERE TO SEE THEM

Te Papa's Te Taiao | Nature gallery displays a skull.

OTHER BEAKED WHALES

Three other beaked whale species are also represented in museums:

Ziphius cavirostris

Auckland Museum's Origins gallery and Te Papa's Te Taiao (Nature) gallery both have skulls.

Tasmacetus shepherdi

This species is now becoming more often seen around Saunders Canyon, off the Otago coast. Otago Museum's Southern Land, Southern People gallery has a disarticulated skeleton.

Berardius arnouxi

Both Auckland Museum's Weird & Wonderful Discovery Centre, and Otago Museum's Animal Attic, display a skull of this rare species.

MYSTICETES / BALEEN WHALES

Baleen whales spend the southern winter gorging on krill in the rich subantarctic waters, but regularly move north from their cold Antarctic feeding areas, past New Zealand, to the warmer subtropical waters more suitable for birthing their calves. On their return journey southwards, many females are accompanied by their older calves.

Humpback whale / paikea / hamupēke
Megaptera novaeangliae

IDENTIFICATION

The body is blackish, and white on the underside and flippers and under the tail flukes. The flippers are very large (5 metres, more than 25% of the body length), scalloped on the trailing edge, and can be smacked on the surface to make a loud noise. These whales are very active, often lob-tailing, spy-hopping, flipper-splashing, and sometimes leaping clear of the water, returning with an enormous splash. The rough knobbly skin on the head is usually encrusted with barnacles. When diving, the tail is lifted to shows the flukes.

SIZE

Adults average 15 metres and weigh 30–40 tonnes. Calves are 4.5 metres and 1.3 tonnes at birth.

NEW ZEALAND DISTRIBUTION

The regular migration route between Antarctica and the northern breeding grounds passes along the east coast of New Zealand in autumn, returning past the west coast in spring. These return trips total some 15,000 km, and are necessary because humpbacks do not feed on their

Humpback whale breaching

mating and calving grounds so rely on packing on enough food reserves while feeding in subantarctic waters to last until they get back. By the time the nursing females leave to return south with their young they will have lost a large proportion of their body weight.

FOOD

Mainly krill and schooling fish. Groups of northern humpbacks have evolved a way to concentrate schools of prey with a 'bubble net'. They create the net by forcing air out of the blowhole while swimming in circles upwards, eventually surfacing through the centre of the school with the mouth wide open. Southern humpbacks more often simply lunge into packed schools of fish or krill.

SOCIAL BEHAVIOUR

Whale songs have long been well known from underwater recordings.

Social groups communicate using long, variable songs, each song unique to one group. On the breeding grounds, males compete with other males, with much blowing and grunting, and sing to attract females and/or impress them. Breaching and flipper-splashing may be statements of strength or location, for communication or for intimidation.

REPRODUCTION

Adults are mature by 10 years old. Gestation takes 11–12 months, and calves nurse for 12 months, so recovery of their numbers is very slow.

POPULATIONS

The humpback's regular migration routes made their seasonal locations easy for whalers to predict. There were once some 50–60,000 humpbacks in the South Pacific, of which about 20–30,000 migrated back and forth along the eastern Australian coast and another 20,000 past New Zealand. In the last days of commercial whaling between 1959 and 1961, more than 25,000 humpbacks were killed in these waters, virtually wiping out the breeding stock. By 2015 there were only about 4,300 breeding around the South Pacific islands, of which fewer than 300 migrated past New Zealand.

Sightings in Cook Strait, made over four-week count periods from shore every year, have recorded numbers varying from 106 in 2012 to 59 in 2013. Now, passive monitoring of singing males by automated acoustic recorders is tracking increasing numbers of whales passing northbound through these waters during the migration period as they recover post-whaling. Australian waters host around another 15,000.

STATUS

DOC See Table 2. IUCN Least Concern generally, but Endangered in Oceania. Protected in New Zealand since 1963.

Humpbacks are vulnerable to entanglement in fishing gear. There were 20 New Zealand reports from 2000 to 2012, 14 of them off Kaikōura. Six of them were released and two freed themselves. Another was recorded in 2018 in the Bay of Islands, and many more in global literature. Maritime authorities, including DOC, have protocols for helping them without risk to rescuers.

WHERE TO SEE THEM

In the field

Humpbacks are often seen from whale watching boats off the Kaikōura coast.

In museums

The Antarctic Discovery Centre in Christchurch has a set of recorded humpback whale songs that can be played on demand.

Antarctic minke whale / southern minke whale
Balaenoptera bonaerensis

IDENTIFICATION

The body is bluish-grey above, lighter below, with a dorsal fin set well back, and conspicuous throat grooves ending before the navel. The rostrum is narrow and pointed, and the baleen plates yellow with a white fringe. Minke whales do not show their tail flukes when diving.

Officially recognised as separate from the common minke whale (*B. acutorostrata*, which is confined to the northern hemisphere), only in the 1990s. There is also a dwarf minke whale, a small southern form of *B. acutorostrata*. It has flippers often marked with a conspicuous white spot, but at the time of writing it is still listed as an unnamed subspecies.

SIZE

Adults average 8–9 metres and weigh 6–7 tonnes. Calves are around 3 metres, and 450 kg at birth.

NEW ZEALAND DISTRIBUTION

Antarctic minke whales are more coastal than are larger baleen whales. They are often sighted in small pods around New Zealand coasts and do occasionally strand (more than 15 strandings have been successfully refloated). Females can apparently be pregnant at any time of the year, but their calving grounds are unknown.

FOOD

Fish, squid and krill collected in Antarctic waters in summer, returning north in winter.

Antarctic minke whale

POPULATIONS

The removal of competition for krill from blue whales has benefited the minke, so their numbers are recovering well. They can sustain a substantial harvest (for example, 98,000 were taken in Antarctic waters between 1857–8 and 1986–7). Since 1986, the International Whaling Commission has permitted Japanese whalers to take 250–300 Antarctic minke whales per year for research. The present southern population numbers about 500,000.

STATUS

DOC See Table 2. IUCN Data Deficient.

WHERE TO SEE THEM

There is a skull on display in Te Papa's Te Taiao | Nature gallery.

Bryde's whale
Balaenoptera brydei

Close-up of a Bryde's whale with its huge mouth full of anchovy

IDENTIFICATION

The body is streamlined and sleek, dark grey above, and paler below, with a small dorsal fin and three prominent ridges along the rostrum (other similar species generally only have one). The throat grooves run along the belly to the navel, and the baleen plates are grey to black. Bryde's whales dive without showing their tail flukes. The name is pronounced 'bru-das'.

SIZE

Adults measure 12–16 metres, and average 12 tonnes. Calves are 3-4 metres, and weigh 900 kg at birth.

NEW ZEALAND DISTRIBUTION

Bryde's whales prefer inshore warm, temperate waters for both feeding and breeding, and are the only baleen whales to avoid travelling to the cold polar region. They are often seen in New Zealand, mainly north of East Cape and particularly in the Hauraki Gulf.

FOOD

Mainly fish such as saury, pilchards, anchovy and jack mackerel, but also krill. By contrast to larger migratory baleen whales, there is no clear separation between feeding and breeding seasons.

SOCIAL BEHAVIOUR

Either solitary, or in resident pods living in loose social groups of 3–6, breeding at any time of year.

POPULATIONS

The New Zealand population is probably under 200, belonging to one of three closely related but poorly defined species groups totalling around 80,000 worldwide. Some 72 individuals are known to live in the Hauraki Gulf, of a local population of 160–200. In those busy waters they are vulnerable to ship strike and entanglement on mussel spat lines.

STATUS

DOC Nationally Critical. IUCN Data Deficient.

Southern right whale / tohorā / kewa / raiti wēra / tūtarakauika
Eubalaena australis

IDENTIFICATION

The body is rotund and almost entirely black except for white patches on the chin or underside, and it has no dorsal fin. The head is very large (approx. 25% of the body), with no throat grooves but an arched upper jaw (hence it is also called 'bowhead') and covered with various lumps or callouses, usually infested with barnacles and parasites. The baleen plates are more than 2 metres long. Right whales are slow-moving, rich in oil and long baleen, and float when dead, hence they were the 'right' whales for early whalers to hunt in rowing boats. The calves are often much paler than the adults, or even white. Southern right whales produce a V-shaped blow, and show their tail flukes when diving. Any cast-up skeleton is easily identified from the high, arched upper jaw and fused cervical vertebrae.

SIZE

Adults average 15 metres, and weigh 55 tonnes, but can reach up to 18 metres and more than 100 tonnes. Calves are 5–6 metres long and weigh about 900 kg at birth.

NEW ZEALAND DISTRIBUTION

Right whales prefer shallow water, and are well adapted to it, so they rarely strand. Adults and calves are regular visitors to New Zealand waters, especially the east coast of the main islands and Auckland and Campbell Islands in winter and spring.

FOOD

Food is collected at the surface by cruising through shoaling plankton

The distinctive calloused head and V-shaped blow of the southern right whale

with the mouth wide open, closing it every so often to strain material through the baleen plates.

REPRODUCTION

Mating is boisterous and competitive, and paternal success depends largely on who can produce most sperm. Hence the testes of adult males may reach 500 kg each, the largest in the animal kingdom. Females mature at around 10 years old. Gestation takes 9–10 months, and the calf is born during winter in a shallow bay. It suckles for 12 months. Pregnant females tend to return to traditional calving areas, which once included many sheltered bays off the New Zealand coast. Few do so now because so many were killed there that the survivors lost that cultural memory, and now calve in and return to the undisturbed waters of the Auckland and Campbell Is. Recently there have been signs that some are returning to former calving sites off the mainland.

SOCIAL BEHAVIOUR

Weaned calves stay close to their mother for 2–3 years. Family bonds are strong, and mothers protect their young from any threat, even from harpoons.

POPULATIONS

The slow swimming speed of the southern right whales made them easy targets for the early whalers, hence they were hunted for their oil and baleen almost to extinction. The estimated total pre-whaling population was 60,000–120,000 worldwide. By 1920, only about 60 breeding females were left anywhere.

In New Zealand waters, the estimated pre-whaling population of between 22,000 and 32,000 was practically wiped out by the 1850s, leaving only about 14–52 individuals by 1923. Recovery has been slow. The total southern hemisphere population is now about 12,000 to 15,000. Researchers from the University of Auckland have created a New Zealand right whale DNA fingerprint catalogue containing over 700 individually identified right whales sampled from around mainland New Zealand and the New Zealand subantarctic.

STATUS

DOC See Table 2. IUCN Least Concern.

WHERE TO SEE THEM

For more information about these whales and their migrations, see www.tohoravoyages.ac.nz. The little-known and unrelated pygmy right whale *Caperea marginata* rarely strands or is sighted at sea. Auckland Museum's Weird & Wonderful Discovery Centre has a model of the head, showing the skin, eye and exterior shape on one side, and the skull and baleen plates on the other side.

Fin whale / finback whale / common rorqual / raratahurihuri
Balaenoptera physalus

IDENTIFICATION

The sleek, dark grey body is white below and on the right side of the head, which is flattened on top. The left side of the head remains grey. The dorsal fin is 0.6 metres tall, set well back, and the flippers small. Fin whales seldom show their flukes when diving.

SIZE

These are the second-largest whales, after the blue whale. Average length is 21 metres in males, 25 metres in females, and weight around 35–50 tonnes. Calves measure 6.5 metres and weigh 3.5 tonnes at birth.

NEW ZEALAND DISTRIBUTION

The main migration route of this species is well offshore, so it is seldom seen. But it is included here because it was once important to the history of Antarctic whaling (p. 144).

FOOD

Fin whales are generalist feeders on krill, fish and squid. They often sweep for prey at the surface, but can dive to over 250 metres.

SOCIAL BEHAVIOUR

The normal social unit has 3–7 members, including adult males. Their low-frequency calls can be heard hundreds of kilometres away.

REPRODUCTION

Adults mature after 6–7 years old. During the southern winter they migrate to warm tropical waters for mating, and the young are born, after a gestation of 11–12 months, in the same area next year. Lactation lasts 6

Fin whale blowing

months, ending when the calf has doubled its length to 12 metres.

POPULATIONS

Fin whales are fast swimmers, reaching over 37 km/h when pushed. One tagged individual travelled, for unknown reasons, 3,700 km averaging 17km/h. They could out-run whalers until the invention of motor-powered catchers. After that, more than 700,000 were caught in the southern hemisphere alone between 1904 and 1979. The present southern hemisphere population is about 20,000, some 10% of their original numbers. They have been protected since the 1970s.

STATUS

DOC See Table 2. IUCN category Endangered.

WHERE TO SEE THEM

In museums

There is an almost complete skeleton in Tūhara Otago Museum's Maritime gallery, prepared from a whale washed up in 1882. It is 17 metres long, complete with baleen plates in life position. Otherwise, they are seldom or never seen close to shore.

Sei whale
Balaenoptera borealis schlegelii

IDENTIFICATION

Similar to the fin whale, but steely grey and with no asymmetry of head colour. It has a large dorsal fin, many conspicuous throat grooves ending before the navel, and small pectoral fins. The baleen plates are black, with fine white bristles. Sei whales dive without showing their tail flukes.

SIZE

Adults are 12–17 metres, and weigh 15–20 tonnes. Calves are 4.5 metres, and weigh 900 kg at birth, slightly larger than the northern subspecies.

NEW ZEALAND DISTRIBUTION

Sei whales are pelagic (preferring the open seas), seldom approaching the coast nearer than the 100m line. There is no regular migration route past New Zealand, so they are rarely sighted from land, but they were once important to the history of Antarctic whaling.

FOOD

Sei whales are fast swimmers, hunting fish, crustaceans, squid, plankton and whatever is abundant and easily skimmed from the surface, amounting to 900 kg of assorted prey per day.

SOCIAL BEHAVIOUR

Adults form firm pair bonds, which may even be monogamous. Family groups gather only at rich feeding sites. Gestation plus lactation total 18 months, so females can breed every other year.

POPULATIONS

In the mid-1960s, Antarctic whalers frequently turned to sei whales

A sei whale at the surface

(150,000 killed from 1910 to 1979) in place of blue whales (when they were protected) and fin whales (when they were depleted). They have been protected since the 1970s, and the southern population now exceeds 40,000, still only about 10% of their original numbers.

STATUS
DOC See Table 2. IUCN category Endangered.

Blue whale and Pygmy blue whale
Balaenoptera musculus and *Balaenoptera musculus brevicauda*

IDENTIFICATION

The blue-grey body of the majestic blue whale has a few pale patches, and a small dorsal fin placed near the tail. The throat grooves extend to approx. 60% of body, and the baleen plates are black. The tail flukes do not show when diving. The pygmy blue whale, a subspecies of the Antarctic blue whale, is similar but smaller. It was distinguished only in 1966.

SIZE

Adult blue whales can reach 25–30 metres long, and weigh 80–190 tonnes. Females are generally larger than males. Calves are 7–8 metres long and weigh 2–3 tonnes at birth.

Pygmy Blue whale

NEW ZEALAND DISTRIBUTION

Blue whales are primarily pelagic (prefer the open ocean), so they rarely strand or are seen from land, but they were once important to the history of Antarctic whaling.

The pygmy blue whale was rarely seen before 2017, but is now often sighted in the Hauraki Gulf between May and November. There is also a population of the pygmy blue whale living in the South Taranaki Bight.

FOOD

Blue whales feed mainly on krill during the feeding season in December–February, especially in areas of ocean upwelling around the edge of the polar ice. They then migrate north to warmer waters for the breeding season after the ice closes the Antarctic feeding areas in March. They can dive deep (to 150 metres) and stay down for 20 minutes. On surfacing, they can blow spray up to 12 metres high.

REPRODUCTION

Calves are born in tropical waters during the non-feeding season. Gestation takes 10–12 months, and calves are fed on abundant (400 litres/day) rich milk, enabling them to double their birth weight in a week. They are weaned at approx. 7 months old, when they are 15 metres long. Females breed every third year.

POPULATIONS

Blue whales can swim fast in short bursts, so were usually able to evade whalers in the days of sail. But after the invention of harpoon guns and steamships, they became the main target of Antarctic whaling fleets in 1925–38, including 29,000 taken from Antarctica in 1930–31 alone. In all, from 1904 to 1967 at least 350,000 were killed. The total surviving population numbers less than 2% of their original numbers. They have been protected since 1967. New Zealand has its own population of more than 700 genetically distinct blue whales.

STATUS

DOC See Table 2. IUCN category Critically Endangered.

WHERE TO SEE THEM

A complete 26.5-metre-long skeleton of a full-grown blue whale, recovered from the beach near Ōkārito in 1908, has long been a key feature of the Canterbury Museum. Tūhara Otago Museum's Animal Attic has a dried single section of blue whale baleen in a wall case.

8. Māori cultural traditions

Pinnipeds

Around 3,500 years ago, the last wave of prehistoric human migration transported Polynesian colonists across the south-west Pacific from Southeast Asia to the Society Islands, and from there to Aotearoa New Zealand by about AD 1280. The huge seasonal aggregations of fur seals and sea lions on their mainland haul-out sites and breeding rookeries offered unprecedented sources of abundant meat to the newly arrived Polynesian colonists. Skilled hunters harvested all accessible colonies of fur seals and sea lions for meat and clothing over the next 150 years.

Moreover, the forest also teemed with large, unwary birds, including nine species of moa (see page 10). These huge supplies of high-quality protein help to explain the rapid population growth of the first settlers. But the culture of their Pacific Island homelands offered no tradition of sustainable management of such apparently boundless resources. Both fur seals and sea lions once ranged right up to the northern North Island, but intense harvesting (page 55) limited their distributions further and further southwards over time.

The people of North Otago and Canterbury concentrated on moa, but those of the South Otago and Foveaux Strait areas looked mainly to seals, especially juveniles and pups. Archaeological excavations at early settlement sites in the far south of the South Island document numerous remains of pinnipeds deposited in early middens (dated to AD 1280–1450), but which are absent from later ones. Within two hundred years, all the living moa plus many other large flightless birds were gone, and the surviving seals and sea lions had retreated to breeding colonies on distant offshore islands.

For example, excavations of the lowest levels of South Island middens dated to the early–mid-1300s found that the estimated weight of pinniped meat represented was, briefly, the same or more than that from moa. In a village at the mouth of the Shag River occupied in the mid-1300s, seals provided almost 40% of the meat eaten there, falling to 12% within 20 years. At Papatowai, the bones recovered represented 12 seals and 10 moa; at Pounawea, 25 seals and 10 moa; and at Tiwai Point, 31 seals and 11 moa. At any one site, this unsustainable harvest would not last long before the community moved on. This early reliance on seals, and the eventual transition to other resources, is clear from the details of timing and location of their remains, strongly suggesting that all local and accessible colonies of pinnipeds were eradicated in turn by Māori hunters. By the mid-1500s, midden sites in the far south were dominated by sea shells, and in due course were overgrown by trees dating from the 1600s.

The bones and teeth of fur seals and (less often) sea lions were important resources for carvers, until the supply ran out at around the same time as did other larger, meaty prey, including moa and penguins. Many cultural traditions and carving themes developed during this early period survived longer than did the animals. See www.doc.govt.nz, and displays in major museums.

The cultural evolution of the skilled Polynesian hunter–colonists shifted from that of their Pacific island ancestors to a new, indigenous Māori system. It was based largely on local adaptations of traditional horticulture and fishing, and reached its classic form as described by the first European explorers in the mid-eighteenth century. Fortunately, the lost mainland colonies of pinnipeds and penguins (but not moa) could be partially re-established from populations on the southern islands that had survived out of reach of Māori hunting technology.

Cetaceans

Stranded whales and dolphins were regarded as taonga (sacred) species, representing the abundance and richness of gifts to the local iwi (tribe) from Tangaroa, the god of the oceans. These great creatures appeared to come ashore of their own accord, presenting their finders with enormous quantities of meat, oil and whalebone. One large sperm whale cast up on South New Brighton Beach in November 2023 was named Te Koha au te ata Hapara, meaning 'a gift from the morning light'.

A carved whale bone hand weapon, a wahaika parāoa

Weapons, fish hooks, harpoon heads and tools were made from whale bone. Auckland Museum's Māori Natural History gallery has a case displaying combs, ornaments and weapons carved from whale bone, plus a video presenting a traditional story recounting a conversation between a whale and a kauri tree.

Some iwi depicted stylised carvings of whales on the internal panels or bargeboards of elaborately adorned pātaka (storehouses) or marae, surmounted by the figure of an important ancestor. One, at Whangara,

This carving of the legendary whale rider is placed atop the marae at Whangara, Gisborne District

celebrates the story of Tohorā (the Māori name for southern right whales and humpback whales) who saved legendary hero Paikea from drowning and carried him to land.

The huge teeth of the sperm whale were especially impressive, and their great strength symbolised the prestige of a powerful chief. A sperm whale stranded on the beach was likened to a chief killed in battle. Teeth from smaller species were used as necklaces and pendants.

The era of European whaling provided iwi living near shore whaling stations with unregulated access to the remains of whale carcasses for their own uses. Skilled Māori sailors welcomed the opportunity to join whaling ships as crew. Their familiarity with the use of spears translated readily into great expertise as harpooners. Less welcome were the supplies of muskets (traded by whalers in exchange for pork and potatoes grown by Māori) that caused huge disruptions of Māori society in pre-colonial days. The inevitable arrival of Norway rats and cats escaping from whaling ships began the assault by invasive species on the native taonga that Māori valued.

Pacific rat, Kiore — an honorary native

The kiore (*Rattus exulans*) is widely distributed on most Pacific islands. Kiore (and kurī, the Polynesian dog) were transported with migrating people across the Pacific in their ocean-going canoes. At the University of Auckland there is a carving in the whare tupuna of Ruanui, captain of the Mamari waka, which bought the ancestors of the iwi of the north (Hokianga) to Aotearoa. It was also carrying a cargo of kiore, three of which are depicted on his shoulder. But whether these animals were loaded by accident or on purpose, or both, is unresolved.

Because the kiore was introduced so long ago, it has been taken into Māori culture. It cannot be included among the true natives because it could not have reached Aotearoa unaided, but it is important to Māori genealogy because its genetics have proven crucial in documenting the history of Polynesian migration across the Pacific, thereby confirming and extending cultural traditions. For example, in the ancestral meeting house Wāhiao of the iwi Tūhourangi-Ngāti Wāhiao, on the marae Te Pākira — Whakarewarewa in Rotorua, there is a carved panel (a poupou) showing an ancestor holding a rat (kiore) affectionately in his hands. It is regarded as the most sacred poupou in this particular meeting house because the tūpāpaku (deceased) of the tribe lie at its feet during iwi and tribal tangihanga (funeral ceremonies).

The earliest presence of kiore in New Zealand by the late thirteenth century agrees with the earliest archaeological evidence for first human arrival, the earliest-dated evidence for widespread deforestation, the

A kiore on a carved panel in Te Pākira Marae, Rotorua

onset of widespread megafaunal extinctions, the pre-European decline of marine mammal populations, and kiore predation on invertebrates. People and their two companions made an immediate and detectable imprint on New Zealand's ecology from the early 1300s onwards.

Māori trapped kiore extensively for food, either in pit traps baited with berries, or in spring snares skilfully constructed from pliant plant stems or dug from under thick ground cover. Kiore were then plucked of fur, cooked in an umu or hāngī (steam earth oven), and, if not eaten immediately, packed in their own fat in kelp-bags or gourd-vessels for transport or for eating during ceremonial feasts.

Kiore bones are present in archaeological sites of all ages around the country, suggesting that kiore must have been widespread from the earliest period of Māori settlement. They were esteemed as food, even though not contributing a major part of the diet. Māori hunting did not eradicate kiore, but both Captain James Cook and Sir Joseph Banks reported them as rare by the late eighteenth century.

On the other hand, kiore were common enough to damage stored food, so one reason for the widespread pre-European use of pātaka (see page 139) may have been to protect food or belongings from kiore damage. Later, pātaka proved a necessary defence against European rats.

9. Whaling in New Zealand waters

The New Zealand Region of the southwestern Pacific Ocean was isolated by vast areas of ocean throughout the last 60 million years, and so was longer protected from human activities than anywhere else in the world (page 11). Whaling on an industrial scale had been well established in the North Atlantic Ocean by 1725, but the earliest European explorers venturing into the Southern Ocean had never seen anything like what they found there. James Cook, and many of those who followed him after 1769, often commented on the huge abundance of whales and fur seals. Better still, in those lawless days these huge, untouched resources were open to anyone to harvest, free of regulations or taxes. The first whalers to break into this Pacific bounty rounded Cape Horn in 1788, and many others followed from the 1790s onwards.

Pelagic whaling

The business of setting up a commercial expedition for pelagic whaling was expensive, in ships, equipment and crew. So, from the beginning this trade was dominated by British and American interests. The earliest whalers hunted whales in their breeding grounds north and east of New Zealand. Harvesting of pelagic whales far offshore was difficult and dangerous, and the early whale-chasing boats launched from modest motherships under sail were slow and vulnerable to being flipped —

Boats approaching a nearly exhausted whale, 1814

chase boat, oars and men — by a wounded whale.

Despite the risks, whalers first targeted the huge, challenging sperm whales. The spermaceti oil stored in the head of the sperm whale had especially desirable qualities that made hunting for them a primary target. Spermaceti oil was a very high-quality fuel that did not smoke or burn when heated, or solidify when frozen, so was ideal for lighting, cooking and lubrication of sensitive machinery in extreme conditions. It was also easy to handle because it could be bailed out of a dead sperm whale's head by the bucketful. European and American markets developed a huge demand for spermaceti oil. At least 30,000 sperm whales were killed by the early sail whalers.

Also, the large teeth in their lower jaws were a valuable source of ivory for carving and scrimshaw (the art of engraving on teeth or bone from marine mammals), a tradition of nineteenth-century whalers carried on by modern Māori carvers. A whole jaw of a sperm whale in the Imaginarium Gallery of the Auckland Museum puts the size of the individual teeth into context.

When the captains of pelagic whaling ships needed to replenish stocks of fresh food and water, or find a temporary base for repairs, they made for the nearest friendly shore, often in northern New Zealand. In 1830 there were 30 whaling ships anchored off Kororāreka/Russell, carrying crews totalling up to 1,000 men. The visits of whaling crews to the Bay of Islands changed the material culture of the northern Māori tribes (page 138). By the 1840s there were more than 700 American whalers working worldwide, most in the Pacific. Inevitably, pelagic whale stocks and profits were rapidly declining by the 1850s.

Shore-based whaling

A less expensive method available to whaling crews based in New Zealand was to establish a whaling station on a shore overlooking a regular whale migration route. In earlier times, huge numbers of baleen whales passed the coasts of New Zealand and eastern Australia, easily spotted by lookouts stationed on clifftops. Chase boats would be launched, and if a kill was made, the crew would tow the carcass back for processing on land. In either case, harpoons and chase boats were at first powered by human effort, which meant that most of the largest and faster-moving whale species were out of reach.

Shore whaling stations often developed into local farming communities providing employment, education, tools and provisions during the off-season. Local Māori permitted their presence, and benefited from the opportunities arising from mutual cooperation. The last operational shore whaling station in New Zealand closed in 1964. The remains of at least 87 shore whaling stations are known and protected as archaeological sites.

Bay whaling from ships anchored in sheltered bays started in about 1827 as the first phase of pelagic whaling was slowing down. Bay whalers

Perano's whaling launch fastening a harpoon to a whale, Tory Channel.

Whaling ship *Tuatea* returning to Fishing Bay, Tory Channel

targeted the slower-moving right and humpback whales for their black oil, boiled down from their blubber, and for their baleen, which was often more valuable than the oil. Between them, deep-sea and shore-based whaling, unregulated throughout the 1800s, devastated all populations of large whales throughout New Zealand waters. By the middle of the nineteenth century, right whales were almost gone, and it began to look as if the whaling era was over.

The harpoon gun

The development of the harpoon gun in the late 1800s, and then the steam-powered chaser, made whaling operations from shore stations or anchored ships much more efficient, and enabled crews to target fast-swimming whale species which had until then been safe.

Until 1904, whales were not pursued into the freezing waters of the far Southern Ocean. Then, when other species became uneconomic, attention shifted to the Antarctic. Over the decade of 1923–33, a Norwegian company ran a series of nine expeditions that set off the last major phase of unregulated and destructive whaling. The Norwegians had been granted a licence by the British government to hunt for whales in the Ross Sea. They came equipped with powerful factory ships that could be independent of shore for long periods, each with a fleet of steam-driven chasers armed with massive harpoon guns with explosive heads. They concentrated first on the biggest species: the blue, sperm and humpback whales. As those stocks dwindled, the whalers moved on in turn to sei, fin and minke whales. They were fearsomely efficient. The total catch over the decade of the Norwegians' annual visits amounted to 18,610 whales. The largest of the Norwegian ships, the *Kosmos,* and its chasers alone took 1,822 whales in the 1929–30 season, and 2,431 in 1930–31, before the slaughter was stopped in 1933. Finally, in the late 1950s and 1960s, the former Soviet Union ran a massive illegal operation taking more than 80,000 whales.

The end of commercial whaling

The International Whaling Commission (established in 1946) now regulates commercial operations. Its long-overdue ban on commercial whaling, which came into force only in 1986, was controversial and is still evaded by some whaling nations. In 1994 the IWC established a circumpolar Southern Ocean whale sanctuary extending from the Antarctic coast to 40°S, which includes New Zealand waters south of about Whanganui.

In addition, New Zealand's Marine Mammals Protection Act 1978 protects all cetaceans in New Zealand territorial waters.

10. Sources and further reading

Baker, C.S. Boren, L., Childerhouse, S., Constantine, R., van Helden, A., Lundquist, D., Rayment, W. & Rolfe, J.R. (2019). *Conservation status of New Zealand marine mammals, 2019*, Department of Conservation.

Cowan, J. (1911). *Pelorus Jack: The white dolphin of French Pass, New Zealand.* Whitcombe & Tombs Ltd.

Dawson, S. and Slooten, E. (1996). *Down-under dolphins: the story of Hector's dolphin.* Canterbury University Press.

Department of Conservation (2007). *Whales in the South Pacific.* Department of Conservation.

Doak, W. (1988). *Encounters with whales and dolphins.* Hodder and Stoughton.

Esler, L. (2014). *Whaling and sealing in southern New Zealand.* Lloyd Esler.

Gill, P. & Burke, C. (2011). *Whale watching in Australian and New Zealand waters* (3rd ed.). Reed New Holland.

Jefferson, T.A., Webber, M.A. & Pitman, R.L. (2008) *Marine mammals of the world: A comprehensive guide to their identification.* Academic Press, Elsevier.

King, C.M. (2024). Biogeography and History of the Prehuman Native Mammal Fauna of the New Zealand Region. *Diversity* 2024, 16(1), 45.

King, C.M. & Forsyth, D.M. (Eds.) (2021). *The Handbook of New Zealand Mammals* (3rd ed.). CSIRO Publications.

Lee-Johnson, E. (1994). *Opo: the Hokianga dolphin.* David Ling Publishing Ltd.

O'Donnell, C. F. J., Borkin, K.M., Christie, J., Davidson-Watts, I., Dennis, G., Pryde, M., & Pascale M., (2023). *Conservation status of bats in Aotearoa New Zealand, 2022.* Department of Conservation.

Peart, R. (2013). *Dolphins of Aotearoa: Living with New Zealand dolphins.* Craig Potton Publishing.

Todd, B. (2014). *Whales and dolphins of Aotearoa New Zealand.* Te Papa Press.

Acknowledgements

Almost all the information given here is derived from the authoritative sources listed above under *Sources and further reading*, and are all easily available through any public library. The primary sources (technical papers and reports) on which the species descriptions rely are not listed separately here, but they can be easily identified from the annotated reference lists available in those publications.

A fully referenced companion paper is published by the author as a contribution to a Special Issue 'Biogeography and Archaeozoology of Island Mammals' in the open access journal *Diversity*. https://doi.org/10.3390/d16010045.

The publisher and author of this book acknowledge with great gratitude the patient labour of all those who have contributed over many years to our knowledge of native New Zealand mammals, and to the curators of all the main museums who provided details of their materials on display (Max Oulton, Zoe Richardson, Colin Miskelly, Paul Scofield, Kene Fleury and Marcus Richards). We are especially indebted to Kane Fleury, who carefully checked the whole manuscript, and Colin O'Donnell, for help with the section on bats.

Special thanks to the copyright holders of illustrations, listed on page 151-153.

I'd like to thank Duncan Perkinson, without whose help this book would not have got off the ground.

Photo credits

All images from dreamstime.com except as noted below:

Title page Dusky Dolphins, Dennis Buurman Photography

Page 7 Topographic map of Zealandia, based on bathymetry data from Scripps Institution of Oceanography, University of California, San Diego. Boundary is based on information which was given in: Nick Mortimer; Hamish Campbell (2014) *Zealandia — Our Continent Revealed*, London: Penguin Books, p. 54 ISBN: 978-0-143-57156-8. This file is made available under the Creative Commons CC0 1.0 Universal Public Domain Dedication

Page 8 Map of New Zealand showing NZ's isolated position in the southwest Pacific Ocean, and the locations of the main and subantarctic islands mentioned in the text.

Page 10 An imaginary scene in a North Island forest a few centuries before humans arrived. Some species are now rare or threatened, and survive only under Department of Conservation protection or on offshore islands; others are totally extinct. Modified by Ellen Clarkson from a painting by Pauline Morse for Wilson, K.-J. (2004). *Flight of the Huia*. Christchurch: Canterbury University Press

Page 17 and 85 Department of Conservation

Page 20 Department of Conservation and Mat Nalder

Page 21 © Whale Watch Kaikōura

Page 26 and 27 Bat Distribution Maps. Distribution of reported locations of lesser short-tailed (left) and long-tailed (right) bats in New Zealand, 2000-2018. From the National Bat Database, compiled by Moira Pryde, administered by DOC

Page 29 New Zealand lesser short-tailed bat in flight. Museum of New Zealand Te Papa Tongarewa, collected 20 June 1998, The Valley, Codfish Island, New Zealand. Gift of Department of Conservation, 1998. CC BY 4.0. Te Papa (LM001330)

Page 30 Lesser short-tailed bat at rest, Eglinton Valley. Photo Colin O'Donnell

Page 31 New Zealand lesser short-tailed Bat in walking mode. Mounted specimen in Te Taio Gallery, Museum of New Zealand Te Papa. Photo Carolyn King

Page 37 Study skins of *Mystacina robusta*. Auckland War Memorial Museum Tāmaki Paenga Hira. LM60

Page 39 Long-tailed bat with wing tag. Photo Colin O'Donnell

Page 41 Wing of a long-tailed bat. Photo Colin O'Donnell

Page 51 and 52 Head of a fur seal, Dunedin 1998. Photo Carolyn King. Fur seals resting on the water, Rottnest Island 2019. Photo Carolyn King

Page 55 Sealing on the Auckland Islands in about 1810. Image in the Public Domain.

Page 58 The male New Zealand sea lion is much larger and darker than the female. Wikipedia

Page 68 Skin and skeleton of Autahi the leopard seal in Tūhara Otago Museum, Dunedin, New Zealand. Image shared with permission from University of Otago Geology.

Page 77 Skull and jaws of extinct dolphin *Squalodon* sp. on display in Tūhura, Otago Museum. Image shared with permission from University of Otago Geology Department by Kane Fleury © Tūhura, Otago Museum, Dunedin, New Zealand.

Page 77 Skull and jaws of extinct dolphin *Waipatia maerewhenua* on display in the University of Otago Geology Museum. Image by Kane Fleury © University of Otago Geology Department, Dunedin, New Zealand.

Page 80 Roadside information board in the Valley of the Whales, near Duntroon, Otago. Photo Carolyn King

Page 86 Distribution of Māui's dolphin. Licensed under the Creative Commons Attribution-Share Alike 3.0 Unported license. Author: Rudolph89

Page 88 Map of Pelorus Jack's regular route accompanying steamers sailing between Wellington (at right) to Nelson across the northern entrance to Pelorus Sound. From Cowan, J. (1911). *Pelorus Jack: The white dolphin of French Pass, New Zealand.* Whitcombe & Tombs Ltd.

Page 92 "OPO" Publicity Caption "Opo" (Known as "Opo George"), the dolphin of Opononi entertains visitors. Photographer N.F.U. Item Code: R24459117. Archives New Zealand

Page 102 Orca Dolphin Blowing: Nathan Pettigrew

Page 113 Pygmy Sperm Whale: Blue Planet Archive / Doug Perrine

Page 115 Beaked Whale stranded on Beach: Blue Planet Archive / Ingrid Visser

Page 117 Strap-toothed Whale, *Mesoplodon layardii* (Gray, 1865), collected 8 November 1997, Opunake Bay, Waiheke Island, New Zealand. CC BY 4.0. Museum of New Zealand Te Papa Tongarewa (MM002917)

Page 139 A traditional Māori hand weapon, a Wahaika, is a short club usually made of wood or whalebone, used for thrusting and striking in close-quarter, hand-to-hand fighting. Wahaika carved from whalebone are called wahaika parāoa. This one dates from about 1900 and is held in the Reitberg Museum in Zurich. This image is in the Public Domain

Page 140 Paikea the whale rider. Photographer: Rob Suisted Image #:15893TN25. Source: www.naturespic.com

Page 142 In the ancestral meeting house Wāhiao of the iwi Tūhourangi-Ngāti Wāhiao, on the marae Te Pākira — Whakarewarewa in Rotorua, there is a carved panel (a poupou) showing an ancestor holding a rat (kiore) affectionately in his hands. It is regarded as the most sacred poupou in this particular meeting house because the tūpāpaku (deceased) of the tribe lie at its feet during iwi and tribal tangihanga (funeral ceremonies). Image reproduced by permission of the elders of Tūhourangi Ngāti Wāhiao of Te Pākira Marae. Photographer Carolyn King

Page 145 Clark, John Heaviside, ca 1771-1863: Boats approaching a whale nearly exhausted / J. H. Clark del; Dubourg sculp. London, H. R. Young,

1814. Alexander Turnbull Library PUBL-0003 https://natlib.govt.nz/
records/23149959?search%5Bpath%5D=items&search%5Btext%5D=clark+whaling
Page 147 Perano's whaling launch fastening a harpoon to a whale, Tory Channel.
Ref: 1/2-C-21773-F. Alexander Turnbull Library, Wellington, New Zealand. /
records/22853600
Page 147 Whaling ship *Tuatea* returning to Fishing Bay, Tory Channel — Photograph
taken by Sanders Photo Studio. New Zealand Free Lance : Photographic prints
and negatives. Ref: PAColl-8163-55. Alexander Turnbull Library, Wellington, New
Zealand. /records/23080690